ALL ABOUT
HISTORY
BOOK OF THE
TITANIC

As the *Titanic* pulled away from the Harland & Wolff shipyard, Belfast in May 1911, she was the largest man-made object ever to be in motion. By the time her maiden voyage began on 10 April, 1912, *Titanic* was also the most opulent, luxurious ship ever to grace the waves. Perhaps what grips us most about this story, and what has continued to do so for over a century, is the vast difference between this ships's potential, the expectations of it, and the eventual tragedy that consumed it. Here you will find the true story behind a tale that has become legendary, from the plans and dimensions from which the ship was born, to the treacherous conditions that would prove its end. You'll gain insights into the lives and ordeals of those on board, the aftermath and quest for justice, and the more recent expeditions to inspect and preserve the wreckage of the ship itself.

ALL ABOUT
HISTORY
BOOK OF THE

TITANIC

Imagine Publishing Ltd
Richmond House
33 Richmond Hill
Bournemouth
Dorset BH2 6EZ
☎ +44 (0) 1202 586200
Website: www.imagine-publishing.co.uk
Twitter: @Books_Imagine
Facebook: www.facebook.com/ImagineBookazines

Publishing Director
Aaron Asadi

Head of Design
Ross Andrews

Editor in Chief
Jon White

Production Editor
Sanne de Boer

Written by
Beau Riffenburgh

Senior Art Editor
Greg Whitaker

Printed by
William Gibbons, 26 Planetary Road, Willenhall, West Midlands, WV13 3XT

Distributed in the UK, Eire & the Rest of the World by
Marketforce, 5 Churchill Place, Canary Wharf, London, E14 5HU
Tel 0203 787 9060 www.marketforce.co.uk

Distributed in Australia by
Gordon & Gotch Australia Pty Ltd, 26 Rodborough Road, Frenchs Forest, NSW, 2086 Australia
Tel: +61 2 9972 8800 Web: www.gordongotch.com.au

All About History Book Of The Titanic Fourth Edition © 2016 Imagine Publishing Ltd

ISBN 978 1785 464 379

Part of the

ALL ABOUT
HISTORY
bookazine series

IMAGINE
PUBLISHING

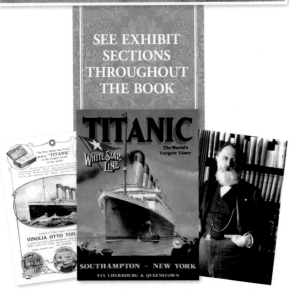

SEE EXHIBIT
SECTIONS
THROUGHOUT
THE BOOK

CONTENTS

INTRODUCTION	7
SECTION 1: GRAND DESIGNS	8
THE AGE OF THE LINER	10
THE CONCEPT	16
SECTION 2: BUILDING SHIPS	22
BUILDING THE BIGGEST SHIPS IN THE WORLD	24
THE GLAMOUR OF TITANIC	28
THE WORKINGS OF TITANIC	38
A NEW COMMAND	42
SECTION 3: THE VOYAGE	46
PREMONITIONS OF DISASTER	48
THREE DEPARTURES	58
ICE AHEAD	64
THE COLLISION	68
MAN THE LIFEBOATS	78
THE BAND PLAYS ON	84
THE RICH, FAMOUS AND UNFORTUNATE	88
W T STEAD	92
THE SHIP SINKS	94
AFLOAT IN THE MIDDLE OF THE OCEAN	104
RESCUED	108
THE SURVIVORS	112
HEROES OF THE TITANIC	116
SECTION 4: AFTERMATH	132
COVERING AN INTERNATIONAL SENSATION	134
THE OFFICIAL INQUIRIES	138
THE CALIFORNIAN AND THE MYSTERY SHIP	142
SECTION 5: THE TITANIC'S LEGACY	154
SEARCH AND DISCOVERY	156
THE EXPLORATION OF TITANIC	160
SALVAGE	164
THE UNSINKABLE SHIP	168
TITANIC REMEMBERED	170
THE ENDURING LEGACY	172
CREDITS	174

❧ INTRODUCTION ❧

Perhaps no ship in history has engendered such continued worldwide fascination as the White Star Line's ill-fated *Titanic*. The largest man-made object ever to have been moved when she was launched at Harland & Wolff's Belfast shipyard in May 1911, within the next 10 months she had also become the most luxuriously opulent ship ever to grace the waves. Everything about her was stunningly impressive, from her remarkable carved and moulded interiors, to the sheer massiveness of her component parts, to her technical features based on cutting-edge maritime technology. Yet, despite design and workmanship that led to her being branded by some as "unsinkable", she took more than 1,500 passengers to watery graves after only five days of her maiden voyage, the result of a collision with an iceberg in the North Atlantic.

Just as *Titanic* had been viewed as the greatest of ships, so did her demise become considered the greatest of maritime disasters. In the days following her loss, the tragedy developed into one of the most sensational newspaper stories of all time, and helped establish the unparalleled reputation for news reporting since enjoyed by *The New York Times*. Her brief life has ever since been the subject of uncountable books, articles, films and other productions.

Even after three-quarters of a century, *Titanic* has proven to be one of the most riveting stories in the world, such as when a team of specialists headed by Robert Ballard of Woods Hole Oceanographic Institution in Massachusetts and Jean-Louis Michel of the Institut français de recherche pour l'exploitation des la mer finally discovered her resting place and returned with photographs of her remains. More sensation was created in the following years when items began to be retrieved from around and even within the ship, and courts ruled her salvage rights to belong to RMS Titanic, Inc.

Titanic still reaches the headlines often, when, for example, the key for the binocular store on her crow's nest went to auction, or when Elizabeth Gladys Millvina Dean, the last survivor of the tragedy, died at the age of 97.

Today, there remains a constant enthusiasm for stories of her background, building, maiden voyage and sinking. Equally as passionately reviewed are the details of those men, women and children aboard her;

of the other ships involved in the rescue (or not) of the survivors; of the official inquiries into the tragedy; and of her subsequent discovery and salvage. With numerous museums, societies and websites around the world dedicated to her story and her memory, there is no doubt that her place in history is secure, and no reason to think that *Titanic* will not continue to be a topic of discussion, research and speculation for years to come.

Neither this volume nor any other likely will ever be the "last word" on *Titanic*. New facts and perspectives are regularly being added to the details of her life, fate and aftermath. But this book adds the special bonus of a wealth of memorabilia, in this case fascinating materials not normally available to the *Titanic* enthusiast. Hopefully, these will help you, the reader, to understand more clearly the luxury and splendour of this grandest of ships and the subsequent magnitude of her tragedy.

BEAU RIFFENBURGH

❧ GRAND DESIGNS ❧

THE AGE OF THE LINER

The era of *Titanic* marked the apogee of transatlantic luxury cruising. In a time before air travel, the grand ocean liner was the most impressive and luxurious form of transportation in the world, the embodiment of both opulence and man's continuing achievement. But the ships that plied the oceans were also the result of competition founded on the burning desire for financial profits.

In 1839, Samuel Cunard won a contract with the British government to provide a fortnightly mail service from Liverpool to Halifax and Boston. Within a year, the Cunard Line had produced *Britannia*, the first purpose-built ocean liner. Soon afterwards, other new Cunard ships – *Acadia*, *Caledonia* and *Columbia* – joined *Britannia* in the first regularly scheduled steamship service to North America, taking approximately 14 days for the passage. For the next three decades, the Cunard Line remained virtually unchallenged.

Meanwhile, the White Star Line, which was founded in the 1840s, developed a strong business taking immigrants to Australia. Within a couple of decades, however, White Star had fallen on hard times, and in 1867 it was taken over by Thomas Henry Ismay. It was not long before Ismay and several colleagues had transformed the company, replacing the old wooden clippers with new iron steamers and entering the Atlantic market. They soon formed a business partnership with renowned Belfast shipbuilder Harland & Wolff,

ABOVE: *Near an old naval sailing vessel is White Star's* Celtic. *Although not as long as* Oceanic II, *at 19,051 tonnes (21,000 tons)* Celtic *was the world's largest ship in 1901.*

which agreed to construct all of White Star's ships. The first product of the new alliance, *Oceanic*, appeared in 1871, complete with numerous design improvements. Within a few years, White Star's *Adriatic*, *Baltic* and *Germanic* had successively won the Blue Riband, the prize awarded to the ship making the fastest crossing of the North Atlantic, and the journey time had dropped to less than seven and a half days.

For the next 20 years, Cunard and White Star battled for supremacy, each successively making faster and more advanced ships to accommodate the increasing number of passengers crossing the Atlantic. White Star's challenge to Cunard did not go unnoticed. In 1888, the Inman and International Line launched *City of New York*

and *City of Paris*. These were not only extremely elegant, but their twin screws eliminated the need for sails while allowing them to be the first ships to cross the Atlantic eastbound at an average of more than 20 knots.

Cunard and White Star quickly responded. White Star emphasized passenger comfort, with Harland & Wolff's chief designer Alexander Carlisle producing *Teutonic* and *Majestic*, the first modern liners. These were ships without sails, with a much greater deck space; accommodation was situated at midships rather than at the stern. Meanwhile, Cunard's focus was primarily on speed. In 1893, the company introduced two new ships, *Campania* and *Lucania*, which promptly won back the Blue Riband.

TOP: *One of the lounges on* Kaiser Wilhelm der Grosse. *With interiors decorated in Baroque Revival style, the German ship was the most plush and ornate yet launched.*

LARGEST AND FASTEST

City of New York and City of Paris were stunning achievements because they were the first liners weighing more than 9,072 tonnes (10,000 tons), while also having the speed to gain the Blue Riband. The following ships are those that held the distinction of being the world's largest liner at the same time as holding the speed record for crossing the Atlantic.

NDL = **Norddeutscher Lloyd**

CGT = **Compagnie Générale Transatlantique**

WB = **westbound;** **EB** = **eastbound**

TOP LEFT: *White Star's* Cedric, *from Will's cigarette card series "Merchant Ships of the World". Ten years after her 1902 launch,* Cedric *took much of* Titanic's *surviving crew back to Britain.*

TOP RIGHT: *Launched in 1888,* City of New York, *had three masts, but never used sails owing to her innovative twin screws. Transferred to the American Line, her name was shortened to* New York.

New competition soon appeared from the Germans, highlighted in 1897 when Norddeutscher Lloyd produced *Kaiser Wilhelm der Grosse*. She was the largest, longest and fastest ship afloat, and one that sported four funnels: a new look that would dominate the years to come.

Not everyone was enamoured of such rivalry, however, as fierce competition did not lead to the greatest revenue. One man determined to put profit first was American financier John Pierpont Morgan. Morgan's goal was to set up an alliance of shipping companies under one banner, allowing them to set rates and eliminate expensive advertising and other competitive costs, thus increasing profits. Between 1900 and 1902, Morgan's investment house and several of his business associates orchestrated a series of mergers and share sales that allowed what became the International Mercantile Marine Company (IMMC) to take control of a number of American and British shipping lines.

The jewel in Morgan's new shipping crown was the White Star Line. Shortly thereafter, a cooperative pact was established with the main German shipping lines. The only major player that now stood in the way of the IMMC having complete domination of the Atlantic passenger trade was Cunard.

ABOVE LEFT: *J P Morgan played a key role in the transatlantic passenger trade, ships were only a small part of his economic empire. He died in Rome, while returning from Egypt, the year after* Titanic *sank.*

ABOVE: *Charles Dixon's painting of the 1899 launch of* Oceanic II. *White Star's new ship surpassed* Great Eastern *as the longest ship yet built.*

AN ORIGINAL BLUEPRINT

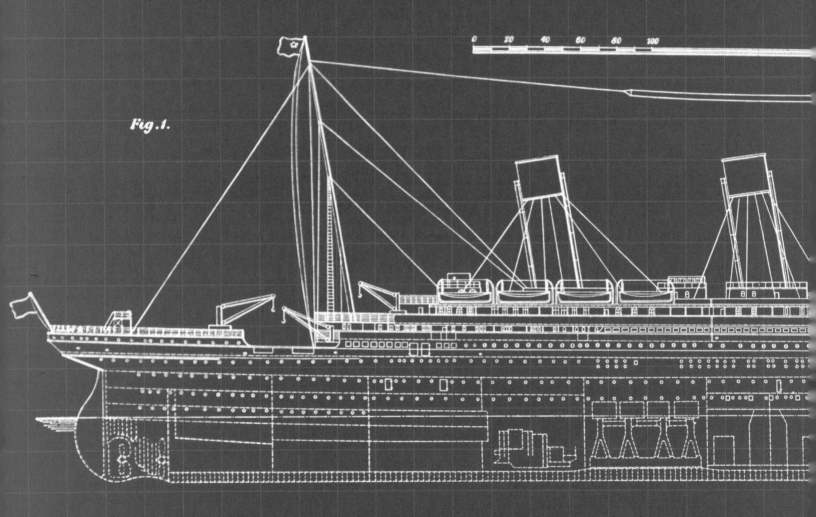

Fig.1.

0   20   40   60   80   100

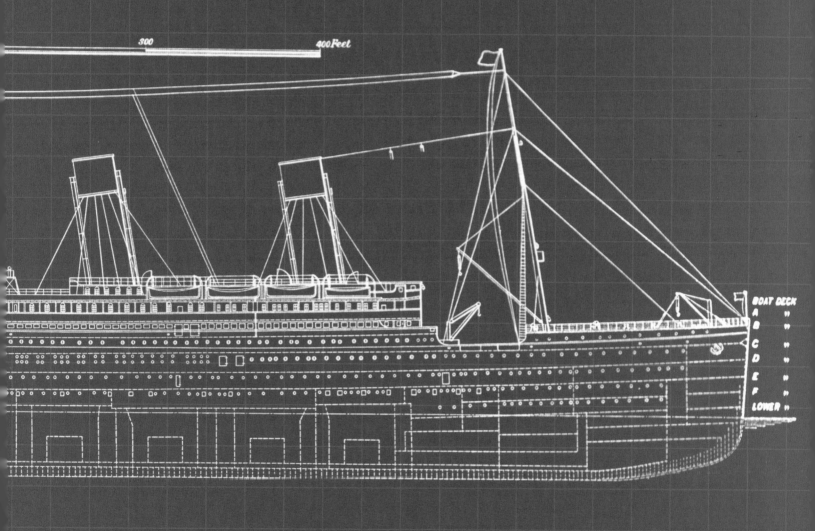

300   400 Feet

BOAT DECK
A
B
C
D
E
F
LOWER

FIGURE 1:
The general arrangement blueprint of Titanic, the most basic of the many blueprints that would have carefully shown the design of every aspect of the ship. The 3-metre- (10-foot-) long original blueprints of the ship's plumbing system, which were taken off Titanic in Cherbourg by naval architect William Wilson, were sold at auction in 2005 for £12,000.

THE CONCEPT

At the beginning of the twentieth century, Cunard, the last major transatlantic shipping line with strictly British ownership, was under threat of takeover by J P Morgan's IMMC, which had already acquired the Dominion Line, Red Star Line, Holland-Amerika Line and, in 1902, the White Star Line. In addition, Cunard ships were being outperformed by Norddeutscher Lloyd's *Kaiser Wilhelm der Grosse* and a new, even faster ship: *Deutschland* of the Hamburg-Amerika Line.

ABOVE: Mauretania *already held the Blue Riband, but when her three-bladed propellers were changed to four blades, she produced a transatlantic speed record (26.06 knots) that lasted for decades.*

It was clear that Cunard needed faster, more lavish ships to compete with the Germans and the IMMC, but the company did not have the funding, so Lord Inverclyde, Cunard's chairman, turned to the British government for help. Set against a backdrop of British unease with growing German power, he negotiated a multimillion-pound loan and an annual subsidy. In return, Inverclyde guaranteed that he would keep Cunard under British control, that the two new ships Cunard built would bring back the Blue Riband and that they would be able to be turned into armed cruisers in case of war.

In mid-1907, the first of these two new liners, *Lusitania*, came into service and, although at 28,622 tonnes (31,550 tons) she was the largest ship in the world, her power was so enormous that she quickly regained the Blue Riband in both directions. Before the end of the year, however, her sister, *Mauretania*, replaced her as largest at 28,974 tonnes (31,938 tons), and also earned the Blue Riband for eastbound travel, proving so fast that she held on to the title for the next 22 years.

The IMMC responded to Cunard's challenge that very year. On the death of his father in 1899,

J Bruce Ismay had become chairman and managing director of the White Star Line. He had kept his position when the company had been taken over, then in 1904 had become president of the IMMC, although J P Morgan maintained the ultimate power.

In 1907 Ismay and Lord Pirrie, chairman of Belfast shipbuilder Harland & Wolff, decided on a revolutionary course of action that they hoped would regain the initiative from Cunard. Their grand concept was to build two huge liners, with a third to follow later.

These would dwarf the Cunard ships, being about 30 metres (100 feet) longer and, at 41,730 tonnes (46,000 tons), half as large again. Rather than attempting to equal the speed of *Mauretania*, the new ships would concentrate on elegance, luxury, comfort and safety, while also still being able to complete the Atlantic passage within a week. Even the lower speed would be beneficial, as it would reduce the engine noise and vibration that plagued *Lusitania* and *Mauretania*. Moreover, the new ships would be so large that they would benefit from economy of scale, their unrivalled lavishness appealing to large numbers of first-class

THE COMPETITION

In order that Cunard could put both new ships into service as quickly as possible, *Lusitania* and *Mauretania* were built at separate shipyards. This resulted in a competitive spirit that saw the shipbuilders incorporate every innovation they thought might make their respective ship the best. Although they appeared similar on the outside, the interiors contrasted starkly with one another: *Lusitania*'s gold leaf on plaster gave it an open, airy feeling, while the oak, mahogany and other dark wood of *Mauretania* produced a more sober, subdued atmosphere. Although *Mauretania* was faster, *Lusitania* ultimately proved more popular with passengers.

Cunard Liner "LUSITANIA" (Turbine).
The largest vessel in the world.

32,000 Tons ; 68,000 H.P. ; Speed 26½ knots ;
Length 787 ft. ; Breadth 88 ft. ; Depth 60 ft.

TOP: *William Pirrie joined Harland & Wolff at 15 as an apprentice draughtsman. Within a decade he rose to head designer. Eventually he became a partner and later company chairman.*

ABOVE RIGHT: *Cunard's* Lusitania, *which, at the time of her launch, was the largest ship in the world.*

TITANIC

...We are in a state of war in the Mediterranean trade, in the Atlantic trade both passengers and freight (the Provision rate being 3/- per ton), and much fear from my latest advices that we are in for a serious upheaval in Australia and New Zealand, but shall do everything possible to avert the latter...

Well, I have undertaken a big job, and look to you to help me all you can, and feel sure I can rely on your loyal and hearty help and support. Again thanking you for your kind cable, and trusting Mrs. Pirrie and you are well, and with my kindest remembrances to both... 99

– J Bruce Ismay

TOP: *The gigantic gantry over the slipways where* Olympic *and* Titanic *were built. It included four huge electric lifts and a remarkable series of cranes.*

ABOVE: *The drawing office at Harland & Wolff, where the plans for* Titanic *were prepared. The many windows and barrel ceiling provided the maximum amount of natural light.*

WHAT KIND OF ENGINE?

One of the key questions for shipbuilders at the start of the twentieth century was whether to power ships with traditional, piston-based reciprocating engines or with the more recent steam turbine. Cunard tested this in sister ships brought into service in 1905. *Carmania's* steam turbine proved faster and more economical than *Caronia's* reciprocating engine, leading Cunard to put turbines in both *Lusitania* and *Mauretania*. Similarly, White Star's *Megantic* used reciprocating engines and her sister *Laurentic* a combination of the two engines. Based on *Laurentic's* success, combination engines were designed for *Olympic* and *Titanic*.

passengers, and second- and third-class passengers also finding larger and better facilities than on any other ship.

The only weakness in the plan seemed to be that there was no shipyard in the world with the facilities to produce such mammoths. That did not stop Pirrie, who simply converted three of Harland & Wolff's largest berths into two specially strengthened and lengthened slipways. Over them, William Arrol and Company, builder of the famous Forth Rail Bridge, constructed a gantry that rose 69.5 metres (228 feet) to the upper crane. Measuring 256 by 82.3 metres (840 by 270 feet) and weighing more than 5,443 tonnes

(6,000 tons), the gantry was the largest such structure in the world. At the same time, Ismay began discussions with the New York Harbor Board about lengthening the White Star piers. He was initially refused, but when J P Morgan began pulling strings, the desired permissions eventually came through.

Meanwhile, plans for the first two ships were drawn up by a team at Harland & Wolff, under the guidance of the general manager for design, Alexander Carlisle, Pirrie's brother-in-law. In July 1908, Ismay travelled to Belfast, where he approved the design plans. The building of the largest ships in the world could now commence.

ABOVE: *Alexander Carlisle, Lord Pirrie's brother-in-law, was one of the key designers of* Titanic, *ultimately being responsible for the internal layout, design and decoration.*

ABOVE RIGHT: *The 16,000-horse-power turbine engine in the process of being installed. This massive engine drove the 20-tonne (22-ton), four-bladed central propeller.*

THE TITANIC IN FIGURES

Length: 822 ft. 9 in.

Extreme breadth: 92 ft. 6 in.

Gross tonnage: 46,328

Engines: 46,000 h.p.

Speed: 22½ to 23 knots per hour

Launch: May 31, 1911

Left Southampton on her first and last voyage, April 10, 1912.

PREVIOUS GREAT SHIPPING DISASTERS

Following are some of the principal disasters at sea that have occurred in recent years:

THE TITANIC'S LARDER

The Titanic took on board at Southampton just before she sailed:

Fresh Meat (lbs)	75,000	Potatoes (tons)	40
Poultry (lbs)	25,000	Ale and Stout (bottles)	15,000
Fresh Eggs	35,000	Minerals (bottles)	12,000
Cereals (lbs)	10,000	Wines (bottles)	1,000
Flour (barrels)	250	Electroplate (pieces)	26,000
Tea (lbs)	1,000	Chinaware (pieces)	25,000
Fresh Milk (gals.)	1,500	Plates and Dishes (pieces.)	21,000
Fresh Cream (qts)	1,200	Glass (pieces)	7,000
Sugar (tons)	5	Cutlery (pieces)	5,000

		lives lost
1911	September 20: Olympic (captain Smith in command) in collision with H.M.S. *Cruiser Hawke* in Cowes Road	–
1910	February 9: french steamer General Chanzy wrecked off Minorca	200
1909	January 23: Italian steamer *Florida* in collision with the White Star liner *Republic*, about 170 miles east of New York, during fog. Large numbers of lives saved by the arrival of the *Baltic*, which received a distress signal sent up by wireless from the *Republic*. The *Republic* sank while being towed	–
1908	March 23: Japanese steamer *Mutsu Maru* sank in collision near Hakodate	300
1907	February 2: G.E.R. steamer *Berlin* wrecked off Hook of Holland during gale	141
1906	August 4: Italian emigrant ship *Sirio*, bound for South America, struck a rock off Cape Palos	350
1905	November 19: L.S.W.R. steamer *Hilda* struck on a rock near S. Malo and became a total loss	130
1904	June 15: General Slocum, American excursion steamer, caught fire at Long Island Sound	1,000

ABOVE: *The original design drawing for* Olympic *and* Titanic. *The plan shows the space given to the boilers and engines, and how the hull was divided into "watertight" compartments.*

		lives lost
1902	May 6: *Govermorta* lost in cyclone, Bay of Bengal	739
1991	April 1: *Aslan*, Turkish Transport, wrecked in the Red Sea	180
1899	March 30: *Stella*, wrecked off Casquets	105
1898	October 14: *Mohegan*, Atlantic Transport Co. steamer, wrecked on the Manacles	107
1896	December 7: *Salier*, North German Lloyd steamer, wrecked off Cape Corrubebo, N. Spain	281
	June 16: *Drummond Castle*, wrecked off Ushant	247
1895	January 30: *Elbe*, North German Lloyd steamer, from Bremen to New York, sunk in collision with the Crathie, of Aberdeen, off Lowestoft	334
1893	June 22: H.M.S. *Victoria*, sunk after collision with H.M.S. *Camperdown*	359
1878	March 24: H.M.S. *Eurydice*, wrecked off Dunnose Headland, Isle of Wight	300
1852	February 26: Troopship *Birkenhead* struck upon a rock off Simon's Bay, South Africa. The heroism displayed by the men on board has earned them undying renoun	454

THE WORLD'S LARGEST SHIPS

The Titanic took on board at Southampton just before she sailed:

	Gross Tonnage	Length, feet	Breadth, feet	Speed, knots
*GIGANTIC	50,000	1,000	110	–
*AQUITANIA	50,000	910	95	23
*IMPERATOR	50,000	910	95½	22
TITANIC	46,328	883	92.6	22½
OLYMPIC	45,324	883	92.6	22½
MAUETANIA	31,938	762	88	25
LUSITANIA	31,550	762	87	25

* Building or projected

BUILDING SHIPS

LEFT: Titanic *was launched in April 1911 in Belfast.*

BUILDING THE BIGGEST SHIPS IN THE WORLD

The first task that now faced Harland & Wolff was to develop the infrastructure that would allow the monster ships to be built. Throughout the latter half of 1908, the two new giant slipways were prepared and the gantry constructed high above them. Finally, on 16 December 1908 at Slip Two, the first keel plate was laid for what would become *Olympic*. Then, on 31 March 1909, next door at Slip Three, a similar keel began to be laid. It was Harland & Wolff's keel number 401, and the ship that would rise from it would become known as *Titanic*.

The two ships were virtually identical in their initial construction. Up from the keel rose powerful frames that were set from 0.6–1 metre (2–3 feet) apart and were held in place by a series of steel beams and girders. Steel plates up to 11 metres (36 feet) long were riveted on the outside of the frames. Each ship had a double bottom, comprising an outer skin of 2.5-centimetres- (1-inch-) thick steel plates and a slightly less heavy inner skin. This was a safety measure designed to keep the ship afloat if the outer skin was punctured. So massive was the double bottom that a man could walk upright in the area between the skins. To hold all this together, more than half a million iron rivets were used on these lower reaches of *Titanic*, some areas even being quadruple-riveted. By time the ship was complete, more than three million rivets had been used.

LEFT: *An advertisement for passage to New York or Boston on the White Star Line ships* Olympic *and* Titanic, *with arrangements to be made through Thomas Cook.*

ABOVE: Titanic *during fitting-out at the Thompson Dock in Belfast. On 8 March 1912 she was towed from the dry dock for the final deepwater fitting-out.*

THE LAUNCHING OF TITANIC

The launching of *Titanic* was a momentous occasion, with an estimated 100,000 people – one-third of Belfast – turning out to watch. J P Morgan, who had come from New York for the occasion, arrived on the chartered steamer *Duke of Argyll*, along with more than 100 reporters from England. Shortly before 12:15pm, Lord Pirrie ordered the last timber supports to be knocked away. Moving under her own weight, in 62 seconds the 21,772-tonne (24,000-ton) hull slid down a slipway greased with 20 tonnes (22 tons) of tallow, soap and train oil. As thousands cheered, the hull slipped into the water until being halted by special anchors.

TITANIC'S SPECIFICATIONS

LENGTH:	269.06 metres (882 feet, 9 inches)
BEAM:	28.19 metres (92 feet, 6 inches)
MOULDED:	18.13 metres
DEPTH:	(59 feet, 6 inches)
TONNAGE:	46,329 gross; 21,831 net
PASSENGER DECKS:	7
BOILERS:	29
FURNACES:	162
ENGINES:	Two four-cylinder, triple expansion reciprocating of 15,000 hp apiece, one low-pressure steam turbine of 16,000 hp
SPEED:	Service, 21 knots; max, approximately 23–24 knots
MAX PASSENGERS AND CREW:	Service, 21 knots; max, approximately 23–24 knots
LIFEBOATS:	16 + 4 collapsible (1,178 capacity)

The original plans produced by the design group under Alexander Carlisle reflected the latest thinking in marine architecture. The hull, for example, was divided into 16 compartments formed by 15 watertight transverse bulkheads. It was believed these made the ships essentially unsinkable, as it was claimed they could float with any two of these compartments flooded. However, the bulkheads were built as a protection against the kind of accident that had occurred in 1879, when the Guion Line's *Arizona* had rammed an iceberg in the fog. Although the bow of *Arizona* was virtually destroyed, the collision bulkheads had prevented her from sinking and she had been able to steam back to St John's, Newfoundland, stern-first. Thus, to many, *Titanic* seemed invincible because her extensive bulkhead system protected her from similar damage; unfortunately, however, it did little to protect the enormously long sides that proved to be the ship's most vulnerable region.

Throughout 1909 and into 1910, more than 4,000 employees of Harland & Wolff worked on *Olympic* and *Titanic*. When Carlisle retired in 1910, he was succeeded by Pirrie's nephew, Thomas Andrews. Finally, in October 1910, *Olympic* was launched and towed to her fitting-out basin to be completed. Work also continued on *Titanic*, and on 31 May 1911, the same day *Olympic* was handed over to the White Star Line, the hull of *Titanic* was launched. Her dimensions were staggering. If placed on end, she would have been taller than any building in the world at the time: 269.1 metres (882 feet) – about four New York City blocks. Even sitting upright she would be as high as an 11-storey building.

After the launch, the hull of *Titanic* was towed to a deep-water wharf, where, during the following months, a giant floating crane was used to load engines, boilers, electrical generators, refrigeration equipment and all of the other heavy machinery needed to run what would effectively become a small town. She received three anchors totalling 28 tonnes (31 tons), eight electric cargo cranes and, far above, four funnels – the three front ones were connected to the boiler rooms, with a dummy aft funnel positioned over the turbine room, to which it supplied ventilation. Carlisle's original plans included only three funnels, but the fourth had been added to enhance the lines of the ship. Each was so vast that a train could be driven through it. With the basic equipment in place, many more months were spent outfitting and detailing, producing what was widely considered the most impressive ship in the world.

❝ For months and months, in that monstrous iron enclosure there was nothing that had the faintest likeness to a ship, only something that might have been the iron scaffolding for the naves of half a dozen cathedrals laid end to end. At last a skeleton within the scaffolding began to take shape, at the sight of which men held their breaths. It was the shape of a ship, a ship so monstrous and unthinkable that it towered over the buildings and dwarfed the very mountains by the water. ❞

- A Belfast observer

TOP: *The vast hull of* Titanic *shortly after it was launched.*

> **❝** I was on the *Titanic* from [when] they laid the keel 'til she left Belfast… Well, I loved it, I loved it, and I loved my work and I loved the men, and I got on well with them all… If you had seen or known the extra work that went into that ship, you'd say it was impossible to sink her. **❞**
>
> *– Jim Thompson, a Harland & Wolff caulker*

TOP RIGHT: *The funnels of Titanic were comparable to other parts of the ship in that their sheer size was simply overwhelming.*

ABOVE: *It took a whole team of horses to pull the specially built cart holding one of the 14-tonne (15½-ton) anchors needed for Titanic.*

THE GLAMOUR OF TITANIC

By the end of her outfitting, *Titanic* had become the most luxurious and elegant ship in the world, and one that could not fail to impress. The designers had even learned from the early voyages of *Olympic*, following which *Titanic* received several alterations before going into service. The major change to the exterior was the addition of a glass canopy with sliding windows along the first-class promenade on A deck, so that the passengers would be protected from bad weather and sea spray.

The interior was extravagantly grand, and first-class passengers were treated to staterooms, public rooms, fittings and furnishings, and food that could be expected from the finest hotels and restaurants in the world. Yet although the ship was strictly segregated by class, it was as impressive for those in second- and third-class as for the wealthier passengers. In fact, second-class bettered that of first-class on most other liners, while third-class surpassed the accommodation and amenities of second-class on other ships.

Each class had its own dining saloons, smoking rooms, lounges or libraries, stairways and promenades. In addition to three first-class elevators, there was one for second-class: a first on

any ship. Nothing was more spectacular than the forward grand staircase (there was also a similar one aft), which was covered by a massive glass dome and extended downwards for five levels, from the first-class entrance on the boat deck to E deck, the lowest level on which there were first-class cabins. Accommodation on A, B and C decks was reserved for first-class passengers, who were also able to enjoy luxurious reading rooms, a palm court, gymnasium, swimming pool, squash court, Turkish baths, their own barber shop and even ivy growing on trellised walls.

The first-class staterooms were decorated in the style of different design periods, including Italian Renaissance, Louis XIV, Georgian, Queen Anne

ABOVE: *An illustration from a White Star Line Brochure of the time, showing how the swimming pool aboard* Titanic *was supposed to look.*

RIGHT: *The splendour of* Titanic *was perhaps best exemplified by the opulent grand staircase.*

FIRST-CLASS SUITES

There were numerous first-class suites on *Titanic*, but the most expensive were the four parlour suites on decks B and C. Each of these had a sitting room, two bedrooms, two wardrobe rooms and a private bath and lavatory. Thomas Drake Cardeza and his mother Charlotte occupied the suite on the starboard side of B deck, paying £512 6s 7d, the most for any passengers aboard; this price also included cabins for their two servants. On the port side, opposite the Cardezas, J Bruce Ismay's suite included its own private 15.2-metre (50-foot) promenade.

and current Empire. They varied from one to three berths, and some incorporated an adjoining or nearby cabin for a personal servant. Many of the first-class staterooms were en suite, but some of the less expensive ones (they varied between £263 and £25 11s 9d) shared a washroom. The 207 second-class cabins, located on decks D, E, F and G, were serviced by their own splendid staircase, and consisted of mahogany furniture in two-, three- or four-berth cabins set off oak-panelled corridors that were carpeted in red or green. Many ships housed third-class immigrants in open berths in large, dormitory-style rooms; although *Titanic* did have some of these (the least expensive fare was less than £7), there were also 222 third-class cabins with pine panelling and attractive floor coverings. For those who were housed in the dormitories, single men and women were kept well separated – men in the bow and women in the stern.

The first-class dining saloon was the largest room on *Titanic*, extending 34.7 metres (114 feet) for the entire width of the ship, and catering for 550 people at a time. First-class passengers could also enjoy an à la carte restaurant, the Verandah Café at the palm court or the Café Parisien, which quickly became a favourite with the younger set. On D deck, the second-class dining saloon, which could seat 394 people, was panelled in oak, like the second-class smoking room, whereas the large

second-class lounge featured sycamore panelling and upholstered mahogany chairs. For third-class dining, there was a 30.5-metre- (100-feet-) long saloon on F deck. Seating 473 passengers, it was relatively basic, and was divided in two by a watertight bulkhead. However, compared with the dining arrangements on other ships, where long, bolted-down benches and crowded quarters were the order of the day, it was vastly superior, featuring smaller tables as well as the luxury of separate chairs.

TOP: *A drawing of a first-class parlour suite. Suites like this were found on both* Titanic *and* Olympic.

CENTRE: *A china serving plate from* Titanic, *an example of the fine crockery used by diners aboard the ship.*

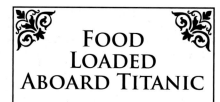

66 We can't describe the table it's like a floating town. I can tell you we do swank we shall miss it on the trains as we go third on them. You would not imagine you were on a ship. There is hardly any motion she is so large we have not felt sick yet we expect to get to Queenstown today so thought I would drop this with the mails. We had a fine send off from Southampton and Mrs S and the boys with others saw us off. We will post again at New York then when we get to Payette. 99

– Harvey Collyer

66 But what a ship! So huge and magnificently appointed. Our rooms are furnished in the best of taste and most luxuriously and they are really rooms not cabins. But size seems to bring its troubles – Mr. Straus, who was on deck when the start was made, said that at one time it stroked painfully near to the repetition of the *Olympic*'s experience on her first trip out of the harbor, but the danger was soon averted and we are now well on to our course across the channel to Cherbourg. 99

– Mrs Ida Strauss

FOOD LOADED ABOARD TITANIC

The food loaded aboard *Titanic* in Southampton prior to departure for the week-long trip included:

FOOD	WEIGHT
Fresh meat	34,000 kg (75,000 lb)
Poultry & game	11,350 kg (25,000 lb)
Fresh fish	5,000 kg (11,000 lb)
Bacon & ham	3,400 kg (7,500 lb)
Salt & dried fish	1,815 kg (4,000 lb)
Sausages	1,135 kg (2,500 lb)
Eggs	40,000
Potatoes	35.7 tonnes (40 tons)
Rice & dried beans	4,540 kg (10,000 lb)
Cereals	4,540 kg (10,000 lb)
Sugar	4,540 kg (10,000 lb)
Flour	200 barrels
Fresh butter	2,725 kg (6,000 lb)
Fresh milk	5,678 litres (1,500 gallons)
Condensed milk	2,271 litres (600 gallons)
Onions	1,600 kg (3,500 lb)
Oranges	36,000
Lemons	16,000
Lettuce	7,000 heads
Tomatoes	2.4 tonnes (2.75 tons)
Green peas	1,020 kg (2,250 lb)
Asparagus	800 bundles
Coffee	1,000 kg (2,200 lb)
Tea	360 kg (800 lb)
Beer	20,000 bottles
Wine	1,500 bottles

ABOVE: *The first-class dining saloon was advertised as the largest room afloat.*
This remarkable venue could seat 550 people and included Jacobean-style alcoves along the sides.

❖ BLUEPRINT ❖

BELOW: A sample blueprint from the construction of *Titanic*,
showing the "additional heater & air pump".

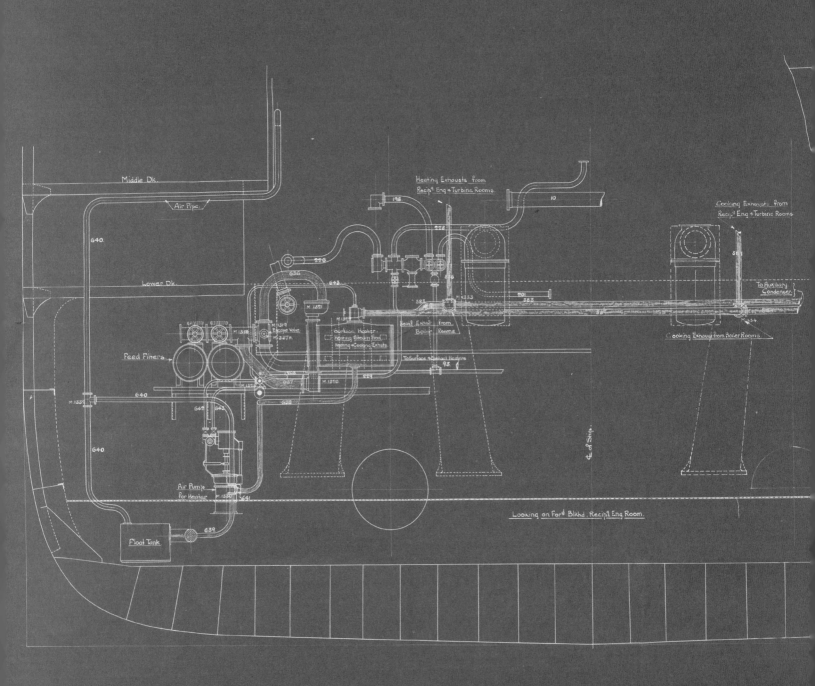

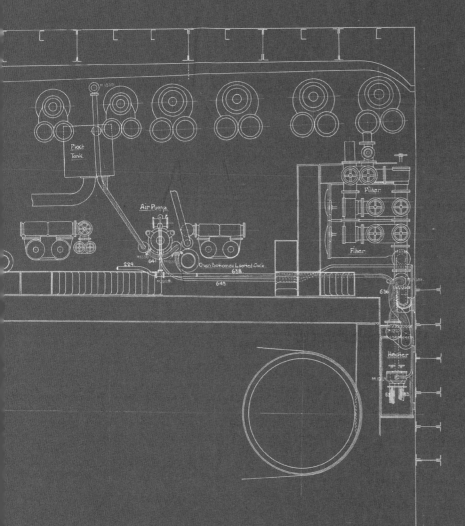

Float
Tank

Air Pump.

Open Bottom & L ported Cock.
638

641

884

643

Filter

Filter

636

Heater

₵ of Ship.

Nº	Description	Bore	Material	IWG
636	Hotwell Pump Disch: Thro' Filters and from Heater (Port Side)	8"	Copper	8
637	" " " " to " (" ")	8"	"	5/0
638	Air Pump Suction from Heater (Port Side)	3½"	"	11
639	" " Disch: to Control Tank	3½"	"	11
640	" " " and Air Pipe	3½"	G.I.	
641	Drain Direct from Heater to Control Tank	3½"	Copper	11
642	Reduced Steam to Aux: Air Pump (Port Side)	1¼	"	12
643	Exhaust from " " "	1½	"	14
583	Heating Exhaust to Heater and Aux: Condenser	5"	"	10
584	Cooking	4½	"	10
586	Heating	3¼	"	12
587	Cooking	3½"	"	11

——— WATER

——— STEAM

—— Nº 401. ——

SKETCH SHEWING POSITION OF ADDITIONAL

HEATER & AIR PUMP.

— SCALE ¾ = ONE FOOT. —

❧ READING ROOM ❧

ABOVE: The reading room on board *Titanic*

The New White Star Liner,
R.M.S. **"TITANIC"**
is the largest vessel
in the world.

It is not only in size but also in the luxury of her appointments that the "Titanic" takes first place among the big steamers of the world. By the provision of VINOLIA OTTO TOILET SOAP for her first-class passengers the "Titanic" also leads as offering a higher

standard of Toilet Luxury and comfort at sea.

VINOLIA OTTO TOILET SOAP

is perfect for sensitive skins and delicate complexions. Its rich, cleansing lather soothes and softens, and for regular Toilet use there is no soap more delightful.

VINOLIA COMPANY LTD.,   LONDON AND PARIS.

❧ SOAP ADVERT ☙

ABOVE: An advertisement for Vinolia Otto Toilet Soap, using the fact that it was stocked on the "New White Star Liner" as a reason for consumers to purchase it. The advertisement only appeared once, in *The Illustrated London News* of 6 April 1912.

COUPON.

AN DEN PASSAGIER: Man reisse diesen Zettel ab und behalte ihn. Nachdem alles Gepäck am Landungsplatz abgeladen ist, reiche man diesen Zettel dem Oberzollbeamten daselbst. Letzterer wird dann einen Inspector beauftragen, die Untersuchung vorzunehmen. Die Beglaubigung ihrer Unterschrift muss persönlich gemacht werden, ehe die Besichtigung des Gepäckes beginnen kann. Alles Gepäck muss für die Untersuchung geöffnet werden.

AU VOYAGEUR: Detachez et gardez ce coupon. Apres que tout votre bagage a ete debarque sur le quai presentez le coupon au chef de douane qui designera un inspecteur pour en faire la verification. Votre declaration devra etre faite en personne avant qu'on puisse proceder a l'inspection de votre bagage. Chaque colis doit etre ouvert pour la verification.

AL PASSEGGIERE: Staccate e ritenete questa cedola. Quando tutto il vostro bagaglio sara sbarcato, presentate questa cedola all' ufficiale doganale dello sbarcatoio, il quale mandera un ispettore per fare la visita. La vostra dichiarazione dovra essere fatta personalmente prima che si possa procedere all' ispezione del vostro bagaglio. Tutto il vostro bagaglio dovra essere aperto per l'ispezione.

Detach and retain this coupon until ALL your baggage is delivered by the steamship company upon the wharf. Then present it to the Customs officer there in charge, who will detail an Inspector to make the examination. Before this can proceed, you must acknowledge, IN PERSON, your signature upon the declaration. All baggage must be opened for inspection.

2—5937

3143SD

Surveys 27.

REPORT OF SURVEY
OF
AN EMIGRANT SHIP.

NOTE.—Cancel the portions of this form that do not apply.

BOARD OF TRADE, SURVEYORS' OFFICE No 403 11 APR 1912 QUEENSTOWN

Name and official number.	Port of registry.	Tonnage.		Single, twin, triple or quadruple screw. Registered horse-power.	Where and when built.	When last been in dry-dock.
		Gross.	Net.			
"Titanic" 131,428	Liverpool	46328 57/100	21831 34/100	Triple Screw	Belfast 1912	Belfast 6-3-12

Date of expiration of passenger certificate.	Mean draught of water and freeboard.	Name and address of owner or agent.	Intended voyage.
2-4-13	34'0" 31.4	Oceanic Steam Navigation Co Ltd 30 James Street Liverpool	Foreign

MASTER AND OFFICERS.

Rank.	Name in full.	Number of certificate.	Grade.
Master ...	Edward John Smith	14102	Ex Master
First Mate ...	Wm McMaster Murdoch	025450	Ex Master
Second Mate ...	Henry Tingle Wilde Chas. Herbert Lightoller	027371 029406	Ex Master Ex Master
First Engineer...	Joseph Bell	19224	1st Class
Second Engineer	Wm Edward Farquharson	32833	1st Class

LIFE-SAVING APPLIANCES.

Description of boats and rafts.	No.	Cubic contents in feet.	No. of persons they will accommodate.	Materials.	Number under davits.	Are they so placed as to be readily got into the water?	Are they provided with the equipments required by the rules?
Boats, Section A.	14	9172	910	Wood	14	Yes	Yes
Boats, " B.	✓						
Boats, " C.	✓						
Boats, " D.	2	648	80	Wood	2	Yes	Yes
Boats, " E.	4		188	Wood with canvas bulwarks		Yes	Yes
Life Rafts ...	✓						

Number of life belts.	Number of life buoys.	Is the ship supplied with all the life-saving appliances required by the rules?
3560	48	Yes

(322a) (61352) Wt.27577/G.143. 1000 11-10 W B & L

❖ BAGGAGE CLAIM COUPON ❖
ᔆ~ᔆ

ABOVE: Even the luggage on *Titanic* was treated well. This baggage-claim ticket had to be presented to the customs officer to make certain that all luggage was inspected upon arrival.

❖ REPORT SURVEY ❖
ᔆ~ᔆ

LEFT: A surveyor's certificate confirming that, as required by the Merchant Shipping Act of 1894, specific spaces on *Titanic* had been inspected and conformed to mandatory standards and could not be used for any other purposes.

No. 657

WHITE STAR LINE.

R.M.S. "TITANIC."

This ticket entitles bearer to use of Turkish or Electric Bath on one occasion.

Paid 4/- or 1 Dollar.

❖ BATH TICKET ❖
ᔆ~ᔆ

ABOVE: One of the most luxurious elements of *Titanic* was the Turkish Baths on board. This is one of the tickets issued for its use.

THE WORKINGS OF TITANIC

As magnificent as *Titanic* was in terms of cabins and public rooms, she was perhaps even more remarkable in areas passengers never saw. Her propulsion came mainly from two four-cylinder, triple-expansion reciprocating engines sending 15,000 horsepower apiece to the massive 34-tonne (38-ton), three-bladed wing propellers. In addition, a 381-tonne (420-ton), low-pressure turbine recycled steam from the other engines, providing 16,000 horsepower to drive the 20 tonne (22-ton), four-bladed, manganese-bronze centre propeller, which had been cast in one piece. This allowed her a projected top speed of approximately 24 knots.

ABOVE: *One of the steam engines, as assembled at Harland & Wolff in May 1911. It was subsequently dismantled and then reassembled aboard* Titanic.

RIGHT: *A group of workmen from Harland & Wolff are dwarfed by the giant wing propellers shortly before* Titanic *was launched.*

THE WATERTIGHT DOORS

Another design feature that led to *Titanic* being considered unsinkable was the set of massive watertight doors linking the 15 supposedly watertight compartments. These doors, extending through each bulkhead, were normally held open by a friction clutch. In an emergency, the clutch could, in theory, be released by the captain using a control panel on the bridge. Each door could also be closed individually at its location. Finally, each door was equipped with a float mechanism that would automatically lift and trip a switch to close the door if water entered that compartment.

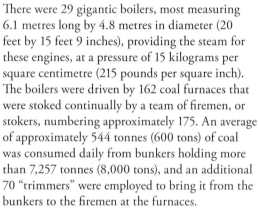

There were 29 gigantic boilers, most measuring 6.1 metres long by 4.8 metres in diameter (20 feet by 15 feet 9 inches), providing the steam for these engines, at a pressure of 15 kilograms per square centimetre (215 pounds per square inch). The boilers were driven by 162 coal furnaces that were stoked continually by a team of firemen, or stokers, numbering approximately 175. An average of approximately 544 tonnes (600 tons) of coal was consumed daily from bunkers holding more than 7,257 tonnes (8,000 tons), and an additional 70 "trimmers" were employed to bring it from the bunkers to the firemen at the furnaces.

The figures were just as amazing for the many other technical features housed throughout the colossal ship. The cast-steel rudder was constructed in six pieces, which together measured 24 metres long by 4.6 metres wide (78 feet 8 inches by 15 feet 3 inches), and weighed more than 91 tonnes (100 tons).

Titanic also benefited from electrical power to an extent that was highly unusual at the time. The main generating plant consisted of four 400-kilowatt, steam-powered generators, which produced 16,000 amps at 100 volts: a total that matched many stations in British cities. But such power was absolutely required because there were no fewer than 150 electric motors, complete with hundreds of miles of wire and cable. These serviced 10,000 incandescent lamps, 1,500 bells used to call stewards, 520 electric heaters, a telephone exchange of 50 lines and uncountable passenger signs, lifts, cranes, winches, fans, workshop tools, kitchen and pantry appliances and navigational aids.

The main plant was also the primary power source for the Marconi wireless telegraphy station. With two dedicated operators, the wireless station was located on the boat deck, where it was linked to a double aerial that ran between the two masts more than 61 metres (200 feet) above the water surface. Considered a key safety feature, it had alternative sources of power should the main electricity go down, including storage batteries directly in the operating room.

The generating plant also powered two refrigeration engines, which in turn drove a host of cold rooms. Separate accommodation was provided for different kinds of meat, fish, vegetables, fruit, milk and butter, beer, champagne, flowers, chocolate and eggs. Perishable cargo was also housed in cool areas near the main provision stores, and cold pantries and larders, ice-makers and water coolers were placed around the ship, where stewards could meet passengers' needs easily.

Even the three-part bronze whistles aboard *Titanic* were something special. Weighing about 340 kilograms (750 pounds) each and standing more than 1.2 metres (four feet) high, they were the largest whistles ever aboard a ship. They were powered by steam via an automated whistle-blowing system that used three chambers with diameters of 38.1, 30.5 and 22.9 centimetres, (15, 12 and 9 inches) for a variation of sound that combined into one sustained blast.

Because of the size and complexity of the ship, communication throughout it had been carefully considered. The boiler rooms, for example, were linked to the starting platform by a series of illuminated telegraphs, allowing the engineer to communicate with them swiftly and efficiently. Overall, the technological achievements of *Titanic* were so imposing that, as completion approached, the trade journal *The Shipbuilder* was able to state she was "practically unsinkable".

TOP LEFT: *A watertight door that was a key safety feature aboard* Titanic.

WHY WERE THERE SO FEW LIFEBOATS?

In 1894, British Board of Trade regulations were established that required all British ships of more than 9,072 tonnes (10,000 tons) to carry 16 lifeboats able to provide space for 962 people. This had not been unreasonable as, at 12,952 tons, *Lucania* was the largest ship in the world. Eighteen years later, however, these regulations had not been updated, despite the fact that at more than 41,730 tonnes (46,000 tons) *Titanic* could take four times that many passengers and crew. Alexander Carlisle was well aware of such safety issues, and his original design planned for *Titanic* to have 64 lifeboats – enough to carry all passengers and crew. However, key figures at the White Star Line or the IMMC insisted on larger promenades, which were gained at the expense of the lifeboats. Carlisle's arguments were overridden, and he was forced to decrease the number of lifeboats to 40, then 32, then finally 16 – with tragic consequences.

TOP: *A detailed reproduction of the bridge on* Titanic. **ABOVE:** *The lifeboats held by their Welin davits at a time when no one expected them to be used.*

❖ A NEW COMMAND ❖

There was never any doubt who would captain *Titanic* during her maiden voyage. Edward J Smith had joined the White Star Line in 1880 as fourth officer of *Celtic*. By 1887, he had earned his first command, and in 1904 he was made commodore of White Star's fleet, for which he generally thereafter commanded the new ships on their first cruises. Smith looked every part the rugged ship's master, but he was also calm, soft-spoken and had such a reassuring disposition that many passengers would only go to sea with him as captain. His crews had equal confidence in him.

In June 1911, Smith took *Olympic* on her first transatlantic cruise, the success of which was offset only by an incident in New York Harbor, when the forces from the huge ship's water displacement pulled the tug *Hallenbeck* under her stern, severely damaging the smaller ship. A similar incident occurred several months later, when HMS *Hawke* collided with *Olympic*, which again was under the command of Captain Smith. These two accidents notwithstanding, when the fitting-out of *Titanic* was finished, it was Smith who was placed in command.

On 2 April 1912, having been delayed one day by bad weather, *Titanic* was put through her sea trials. Aboard were 41 officers and senior crew and 78 men from the "black gang": stokers, trimmers and greasers. Harold Sanderson represented the White Star Line and Thomas Andrews was there for Harland & Wolff, as was his "Guarantee Group": a select company of eight enthusiastic and extremely talented men who went on maiden voyages to resolve any problems that arose. Throughout the day, *Titanic's* speed, turning and manoeuvring capability, stopping distance, reversing and many other functions, including wireless, anchors and electrical systems, were tested. That evening, she was approved by the Board of Trade and transferred over to White Star.

Intriguingly, this approval was given despite a fire smouldering in a boiler-room coal bunker. Although fire is normally the most feared danger aboard ship, the problem could not be immediately controlled, and it was in fact a number of days before the bunker had been emptied to the extent that the seat of the blaze could be extinguished.

COLLISION WITH HMS HAWKE

Even a master with Edward Smith's experience had much to learn about handling giant liners. On 20 September 1911, *Olympic* departed from Southampton on her fifth voyage. After sailing on a course parallel to HMS *Hawke*, *Olympic* turned, and the 6,804-tonne (7,500-ton) naval cruiser rammed into her, puncturing her in two places. It was later determined that dynamic forces caused by massive water displacement had pulled *Hawke* into *Olympic*, and the harbour pilot, rather than Smith, received the official blame. Meanwhile, *Olympic's* repairs in Belfast assumed priority over work on *Titanic*, thereby delaying *Titanic's* first cruise for three weeks.

LEFT: *Interested bystanders watch as workmen investigate the damage to* Olympic *caused by the collision with HMS* Hawke. *Both ships were seriously damaged, but no people were injured.*

At 8pm, after boarding fresh provisions, *Titanic* left Belfast for the last time, steaming for Southampton. En route, she reached a speed of 23 knots – the fastest she would ever go. When she arrived at Southampton shortly before midnight on 3 April, she swung round and, with the help of several tugs, approached the dock stern-first. She would thus be able to make an impressive departure without having to turn while leaving. There were now only six days for provisioning and staffing, and for making any final touches in preparation for the maiden voyage. One of the most demanding tasks was coaling, because a national coal strike ended only on 6 April, four days before her scheduled departure. With no time for coal to arrive from the pits, White Star transferred 4,016 tonnes (4,427 tons) from five other International Mercantile Marine Company ships in port and from the stock remaining after

the departure of *Olympic*, which had left only hours before *Titanic* arrived.

One unexpected addition to the ship in Southampton was that of Henry T Wilde, who was named chief officer after having served in the same position aboard *Olympic*. The other officers had joined in Belfast with Captain Smith, but late in the game it was decided that Wilde's hands-on knowledge of the vast new ocean liners meant he should be aboard for *Titanic's* first voyage. The current chief officer, William Murdoch, was dropped to first officer, and first officer Charles Lightoller became the second officer. The third through sixth officers – Herbert Pitman, Joseph Boxhall, Harold Lowe and James Moody – remained the same, while the second officer who had joined in Belfast, a man by the name of David Blair, was reassigned elsewhere, not yet knowing his extremely good fortune.

> **"We have made a good run from Southampton everything working A1, we nearly had a collision with the *New York* and *Oceanic* when leaving…, the wash of our propellers made the two ships range about when we were passing them, this made their mooring ropes break and the *New York* set off across the river until the tugs got hold of her again, no damage was done but it looked like trouble at the time. "**
>
> – *Joseph Bell in a letter sent to his son Frank from onboard* Titanic

---

TOP LEFT: *One of the biggest tasks for the crew in port was to bring aboard and unload the post. Also shown is a crewman adjusting a lantern.*

TOP RIGHT: *Purser Hugh McElroy and Captain Edward J Smith aboard* Titanic *before her final stop at Queenstown, Ireland. Neither man survived the tragedy.*

ABOVE: *At the age of 51, chief engineer Joseph Bell was a highly respected professional who had spent about 27 years with White Star Line.*

THE CREW OF TITANIC

Just as there is debate about the exact number of passengers saved and lost on *Titanic*, there is no agreement about the exact number of serving crew, although they numbered approximately 890. Recent estimates for the crew by department and position include:

DEPARTMENT	TOTAL
Victualling Department	431
Saloon Stewards	130
Bedroom Stewards	47
Stewards	46
Cooks and Bakers	34
Stewardesses	21
Scullions	13
Assistant Saloon Stewards	13
Engine Department	325
Firemen/Stokers	161
Trimmers	72
Greasers	33
Leading Firemen	13
À la Carte Restaurant Department	69
Assistant Waiters	17
Waiters	16
Cooks	15
Deck Department	66
Able Seamen	29

❝When anyone asks how I can best describe my experience in nearly 40 years at sea, I merely say, uneventful. Of course there have been winter gales, and storms and fog the like, but in all my experience, I have never been in any accident of any sort worth speaking about... I never saw a wreck and never have been wrecked, nor was I ever in any predicament that threatened to end in disaster of any sort. You see, I am not very good material for a story❞

– Captain Smith

TOP RIGHT: *Captain Smith (centre, with the white beard) with his senior officers aboard* Titanic.

ABOVE: *Vendors had franchises to sell lace and other souvenirs aboard liners at Queenstown, as shown in one of the last photos from* Titanic, *taken by Father Browne.*

THE VOYAGE

RIGHT: Titanic *leaving Southampton bound for New York after stops in France and Belfast.*

PREMONITIONS OF DISASTER

Perhaps the eeriest aspect of the *Titanic* disaster was the large number of prophetic tales and premonitions that seemed to foretell its terrible fate. As early as 1886, the famed British journalist W T Stead wrote a fictional story entitled "How the Mail Steamer Went Down in Mid-Atlantic" for his newspaper, *The Pall Mall Gazette*. In the story, a liner sank after colliding with another ship, and most of the people aboard died because of a shortage of lifeboats. At the end of the piece, Stead added: "This is exactly what might take place and will take place if liners are set free short of boats." Six years later, in *Review of Reviews*, Stead revisited the theme in another short work of fiction, "From the Old World to the New", in which a clairvoyant aboard White Star's *Majestic* helped to guide a rescue of those aboard another ship that had struck an iceberg in the North Atlantic. Uncannily, the name Stead gave to the captain of *Majestic* was E J Smith – the same name as the captain of *Titanic*. Even stranger, Stead lost his life as a first-class passenger on *Titanic*.

In 1898, 14 years before the tragedy, the former merchant navy officer Morgan Robertson published the novella *The Wreck of the Titan; or, Futility*, in which an "unsinkable" British liner named *Titan*, on a voyage from New York to England, sank with 2,000 people aboard after being tipped on her side in a collision with an iceberg. Not only was the description of *Titan* unnervingly similar to *Titanic* – having roughly the same length, displacement, speed, watertight compartments and number of propellers – but the fictional ship also lacked anywhere near the proper number of lifeboats.

Equally as bizarre were the numerous portentous events surrounding people sailing on *Titanic*. One of the most fortunate of those to embark was Father Frank Browne, a theology student in Dublin. On 4 April 1912, he received an unexpected present from his uncle, the Bishop of Cloyne: a first-class ticket for the initial two stops on *Titanic*'s maiden voyage, from Southampton to Cherbourg to Queenstown, Ireland. While aboard, Browne was befriended by a wealthy American, who offered to pay his passage to New York. When Browne asked his Jesuit superiors for permission, he received the no-nonsense reply: "Get off that ship." Browne followed his concerned supervisor's

ABOVE: *An older Father Frank Browne. His later photographic achievements were widely respected.*

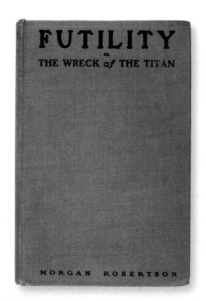

NO POPE

Although many consider one story that originated during the building of *Titanic* to be a myth, it remains one of the most often-repeated tales. It is said that the number 3909 04 was scrawled on the hull as an addition to its official hull number, 401. When this was seen one day as a mirror image, it was noted with horror that it read "NO POPE". Many of the workers in Belfast were Catholic, and it is rumoured that there was great anxiety and concern among them, which later turned to certainty that the ship was destined for disaster.

TOP: *An old copy of Morgan Robertson's classic disaster novella, which was originally published with the two parts of the title in the reverse order.*

ABOVE: *Father Browne shot this image of crowds at the White Star Wharf in Queenstown waiting to embark the tenders that would take them to* Titanic.

instruction, and within just a few days found that the numerous photographs he had taken aboard *Titanic* became famous as the last ones of the doomed ship.

Others with apprehensive relatives or friends were not so fortunate. John Hume, the Scottish violinist who was one of *Titanic*'s eight-man orchestra, had been aboard *Olympic* during the collision with HMS *Hawke*. This had unnerved his mother terribly, and she begged her 28-year-old son not to sail on *Titanic* after a dream told her of terrible consequences. Such a decision could have made gaining future employment with White Star difficult, so Hume boarded with the other musicians at Southampton – and all of them lost their lives. Similarly, Broadway producer Henry B Harris ignored the impassioned pleas of his business associate William Klein not to

sail on *Titanic*, and he and his wife embarked in Southampton. Four days later, Mrs Harris was able to enter a lifeboat, but her husband paid the ultimate price.

There were numerous other confirmed instances of foreboding about a tragedy, which were or were not heeded by those scheduled to board. The latest addition to the litany of premonitions was made public only as recently as March 2007, when it was revealed that Alfred Rowe, a Liverpudlian businessman who also owned a ranch in Texas, posted a letter to his wife from Queenstown. Citing the near-collision with *New York* during the departure from Southampton, he told her that *Titanic* was too large, that she was a "positive danger", and that, were he still able to change, he would rather be on *Mauretania* or *Lusitania*. Rowe died in the disaster.

JOHN PIERPONT MORGAN – SURVIVOR

Perhaps the most mysterious cancellation for *Titanic* was made by none other than J P Morgan. At one point Morgan was scheduled to occupy the glamorous port promenade suite on B Deck. However, he cancelled his reservation, claiming, according to some sources, that his business interests required him to remain in Europe. Others indicated that Morgan backed out owing to ill health. However, two days after the tragedy, a reporter found him in a French spa town, healthy and happy in the company of his mistress. The suite was taken instead by J Bruce Ismay.

TOP: *Another photograph taken by Father Browne shows an American Medical official inspecting passengers' eyes before allowing them aboard. No one suffering from trachoma was permitted to travel to the US.*

BOX: *The incredibly successful banker J P Morgan managed to avoid the* Titanic *disaster as he cancelled his stay.*

RIGHT: *Frank Browne took this photo of the sunrise from aboard* Titanic *near Land's End in Cornwall, while transiting from Cherbourg to Queenstown on 11 April.*

WHITE STAR LINE.

JAMES SCOTT & C<u>o</u>. Agents.

1, COCKSPUR STREET. S.W.
"Oceanic House."
TELEGRAPHIC ADDRESS: "VESSELS, LONDON."

38, LEADENHALL STREET, E.C.
LONDON.
TELEGRAPHIC ADDRESS: "ISMAY, LONDON."

CANUTE ROAD, SOUTHAMPTON.
TELEGRAPHIC ADDRESS: "ISMAY, SOUTHAMPTON."

9, BROADWAY, NEW YORK.
TELEGRAPHIC ADDRESS: "ISMAY, NEW YORK."

84, STATE ST. BOSTON.
TELEGRAPHIC ADDRESS: "ISMAY, BOSTON."

118, NOTRE DAME ST. WEST, MONTREAL.
TELEGRAPHIC ADDRESS: "ISMAY, MONTREAL."

21, PIAZZA DELLA BORSA, NAPLES.
TELEGRAPHIC ADDRESS: "ISMAY, NAPLES."

VIA ALLA NUNZIATA, N<u>o</u> 18, GENOA.
TELEGRAPHIC ADDRESS: "ISMAY, GENOA."

PARIS AGENT: NICHOLAS MARTIN, 9, RUE SCRIBE.
TELEGRAPHIC ADDRESS: "ISMAY, PARIS."

30, JAMES ST., LIVERPOOL.
TELEGRAPHIC ADDRESS: "ISMAY, LIVERPOOL."

Telegrams: "ISMAY." Queenstown.
Telephone N<u>o</u> 3.

Passenger. Department.

Scott's Square,
QUEENSTOWN, April 3rd. 19 12.

OLYMPIC (TRIPLE SCREW) 45,324 TONS
TITANIC (TRIPLE SCREW) 45,000 TONS
THE LARGEST STEAMERS IN THE WORLD

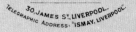

**WHITE STAR LINE
SERVICES.**

SOUTHAMPTON-CHERBOURG-NEW YORK.
ROYAL & UNITED STATES MAIL STEAMERS.
VIA QUEENSTOWN (WESTBOUND)-PLYMOUTH (EASTBOUND)

LIVERPOOL-NEW YORK.
VIA QUEENSTOWN.

LIVERPOOL-NEW YORK.
(FREIGHT.)

LIVERPOOL-BOSTON.
VIA QUEENSTOWN.

LIVERPOOL-QUEBEC-MONTREAL.

LIVERPOOL-AUSTRALIA.
VIA SOUTH AFRICA.

LIVERPOOL-AUSTRALIA.
(FREIGHT.)

LIVERPOOL-NEW ZEALAND.
(FREIGHT.)

LONDON-NEW ZEALAND.
VIA SOUTH AFRICA.

NEW YORK-MEDITERRANEAN.
VIA AZORES.

BOSTON-MEDITERRANEAN.
VIA AZORES.

THROUGH BOOKINGS
TO ALL PARTS
OF THE WORLD.

Dear Father Browne,   "<u>First Class</u>"

      We have pleasure in handing you

herewith pass from Southampton to Queenstown per

s.s. "Titanic" April 10th, and we trust you will have

an enjoyable trip.

           Yours truly,

           FOR JAMES SCOTT & Co.,

The Rev. F. M. Browne. S. J.

      Bishop's Palace,

        Queenstown.

 FATHER BROWN TICKET

ABOVE: A letter that accompanied the cruise ticket of Father Frank Browne, from James Scott & Co, agents for White Star Line.

❧ CAPTAIN J E SMITH ❧

ABOVE: Captain John Edward Smith looks down at the first tender approaching to disembark passengers at Queenstown.

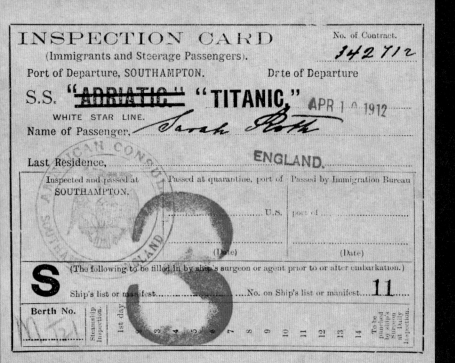

❖ INSPECTION CARD ❖

LEFT: An inspection card issued to one of the third class passengers.

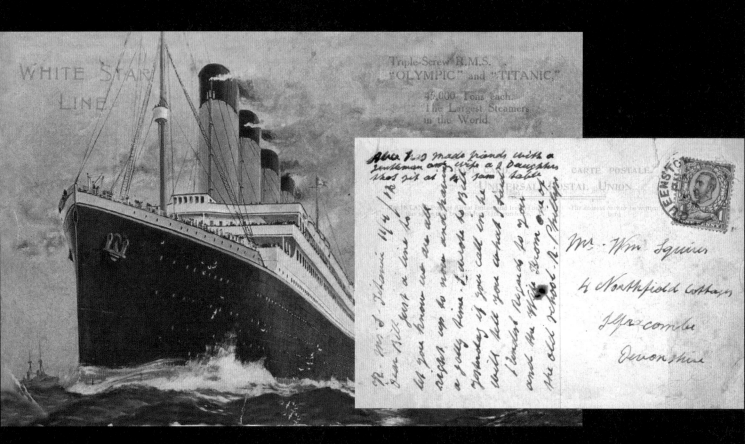

❖ POSTCARD AT QUEENSTOWN ❖

ABOVE: A postcard sent from Queenstown by Escott Robert Phillips, a second-class passenger, to his friend Bill Squires. Phillips died when the ship sank, but his 21-year-old daughter Alice escaped in Lifeboat 12.

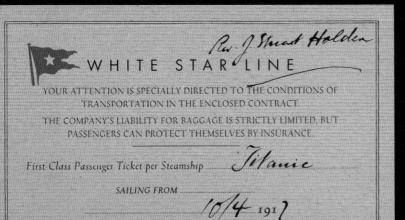

❖ FIRST CLASS TICKET ❖

LEFT: A rare first class ticket for the maiden voyage of *Titanic*.

ICEBERG SKETCH

ABOVE: A sketch made by Joseph Scarrott, a surviving crew member who drew the iceberg from memory, noting its shape resembled the Rock of Gibraltar.

ISSUED BY THE
BOARD OF TRADE.

SURVEY OF AN EMIGRANT SHIP.

No 408
BOARD OF TRADE, SURVEYORS OFFICE
13 APR. 1912
QUEENSTOWN

Certificate for Clearance.

Ship's Name and Official Number. (1.)	Port of Registry, and Tonnage. (2.)		Name of Master. (3.)
Titanic 131428	L'pool Gross. 46328	Register. 21831	E.J. Smith.

Port of Departure. (4.)	Ports of Call. (5.)	Destination. (6.)
Southampton	Cherbourg and Queenstown	New York

CABIN PASSENGERS.

Adults (12 years and upwards).				Children.				Total Cabin Passengers. (15.)	Equal to Adults computed by Part III. M. S. Act, 1894. (16.)	
Married.		Single.		Between 1 and 12.		Under 1 Year.				
Male. (7.)	Female. (8.)	Male. (9.)	Female. (10.)	Male. (11.)	Female. (12.)	Male. (13.)	Female. (14.)			Single
52	52	196	101	10	12	4	—	427	412	Chbd
29	29	151	58	3	2	—	—	172	169½	2:slon
		5	2					7	7	

STEERAGE PASSENGERS.*

Adults (12 years and upwards).				Children.				Total Steerage Passengers. (25.)	Equal to Adults computed by Part III. M. S. Act, 1894. (26.)	
Married.		Single.		Between 1 and 12.		Under 1 Year.				
Male. (17.)	Female. (18.)	Male. (19.)	Female. (20.)	Male. (21.)	Female. (22.)	Male. (23.)	Female. (24.)			Single
25	25	313	74	22	28	3	3	495	464	Chbd
4	4	59	18	2	—	3	—	182	92½	2'slon
2	2	50	54	—	—	—	—	113	110½	

CREW.

Deck Department. (27.)	Engine Department. (28.)	Stewards' Department. (29.)	Total Crew. (30.)	Equal to Adults computed by Part III. M. S. Act, 1894. (31.)
73	325	494	892	892

Total Number actually on board, including Crew	2208	2147

* Total Number of Statute Adults (as Steerage Passengers), exclusive of the Master, Crew, and Cabin Passengers, which the Ship can legally carry according to space allotted	Clear Space in Sq. Ft.	Number of Beds fitted.
1735	26992	1134

I hereby certify that the particulars inserted in the above form are correct. I also certify that all the requirements of the Merchant Shipping Acts relating to emigrant ships, so far as they can be complied with before the departure of the ship, have been complied with, and that the ship is, in my opinion, seaworthy, in safe trim, and in all respects fit for her intended voyage; that she does not carry a greater number of passengers than in the proportion of one statute adult to every five superficial feet of space clear for exercise on deck; and that her passengers and crew are ... the Ship a fit state to proceed.

Dated at Queenstown

this 11th day of April 19 12

E.J. Sharpe

Emigration Officer, or Assistant Emigration Officer.

(238M) (62245) Wt. 30276/150 3000 12-10 W B & L

❦ CLEARANCE FORM ❦

〜❦〜

ABOVE: The Certificate of Clearance as an "Emigrant ship" for *Titanic* to depart from Southampton. Note that it is dated 11 April.

Form No. 4.—100— 17.8.10.

Deld. Date _14 Apr 1912_

The Marconi International Marine Communication Co., Ltd.,
WATERGATE HOUSE, YORK BUILDINGS, ADELPHI, LONDON, W.C.

No. "OLYMPIC"   OFFICE.   14 Apr   19 12

CHARGES TO PAY.

Handed in at ___TITANIC___

This message has been transmitted subject to the conditions printed on the back hereof, which have been agreed to by the Sender. If the accuracy of this message be doubted, the Receiver, on paying the necessary charges, may have it repeated whenever possible, from Office to Office over the Company's system, and should any error be shown to exist, all charges for such repetition will be refunded. This Form must accompany any enquiry respecting this Telegram.

Total

To   OLYMPIC

Eleven pm NEW YORK TIME   TITANIC SENDING OUT SIGNALS OF DISTRESS

ANSWERED HIS CALLS.

TITANIC REPLIES AND GIVES ME HIS POSITION 41.46 N 50 14 W AND SAYS

"WE HAVE STRUCK AN ICE BERG".

OUR DISTANCE FROM TITANIC 505 MILES.

Form No. 4.—100— 17.8.10.

Deld. Date 15 ABR 1912

The Marconi International Marine Communication Co., Ltd.,
WATERGATE HOUSE, YORK BUILDINGS, ADELPHI, LONDON, W.C.

No. OLYMPIC   OFFICE.   15 ABR 1912   19

CHARGES TO PAY.

     C A R P A T H I A

Handed in at ___

This message has been transmitted subject to the conditions printed on the back hereof, which have been agreed to by the Sender. If the accuracy of this message be doubted, the Receiver, on paying the necessary charges, may have it repeated whenever possible, from Office to Office over the Company's system, and should any error be shown to exist, all charges for such repetition will be refunded. This Form must accompany any enquiry respecting this Telegram.

Total

To

OLYMPIC   Received 2.10 pm   N.Y.T.

WE RECEIVED DISTRESS SIGNAL CALL FROM THE TITANIC AT ELEVEN TWENTY AND
PROCEEDED RIGHT TO SPOT MENTIONED. ON ARRIVAL AT DAYBREAK WE SAW
ICE 25 MILES LONG APPARENTLY SOLID, QUANTITY OF WRECKAGE AND NUMBER
OF BOATS FULL OF LIVES. WE RAISED ABOUT SIX HUNDRED AND SEVENTY SOULS.
TITANIC HAS SUNK SHE WENT DOWN IN TWO HOURS. CAPTAIN AND ALL ENGINEERS
OUR CAPTAIN SENT ORDER THAT THERE WAS NO NEED FOR BALTIC TO COME ANY
FURTHER SO WITH THAT SHE RETURNED ON HER COURSE TO LIVERPOOL.
WE HAVE TWO OR THREE OFFICERS ABOARD AND THE SECOND MARCONI OPERATOR
WHO HAD BEEN CREEPING HIS WAY THROUGH WATER AT 30 DEGREES FOR SEVERAL
HOURS. MR. ISMAY IS ABOARD.

❧ TELEGRAMS ❧

ABOVE: This tragic series of six telegrams shows the desperate correspondence between
Titanic and *Olympic*, and then — when it is too late — between *Carpathia* and *Olympic*.

THREE DEPARTURES

Wednesday, 10 April dawned fair and breezy. Throughout Southampton, hundreds of crew headed for Berth 44 at the dockyard, where at 6am they were directed to their quarters aboard *Titanic* prior to general muster. Three and a half hours later, another massive influx occurred as most of the second- and third-class passengers arrived on the boat train from Waterloo Station, and were then guided to their separate entrances to the ship. At 11:30am, scarcely half an hour before departure, another train arrived, this time holding first-class passengers, who were efficiently escorted to their staterooms. Promptly at noon, with hundreds of family members, well-wishers and spectators waving and cheering from the quayside, three loud blasts announced departure. The sound had hardly stopped reverberating through the air before disaster nearly struck.

Having been pulled out of the enclosed dock area by five tugs, *Titanic* began to move slowly – and then more rapidly – along the River Test. The turbulence caused by the forward motion of a ship with such incredible size and draft was dissipated harmlessly into the river on her starboard side. But on her port side, the displaced water was trapped between the monstrous ship and the dock's bulkheads. Tied in tandem at Berth 38 were two liners, *Oceanic* and *New York*, that were out of service until they could be coaled.

As *Titanic* swept near them, the displaced water caused *New York* to bounce up and down with such violence that all six of her mooring lines snapped. And as *Titanic* continued, the waves in her wake drew the stern of the now-free *New York* in an arc towards her. George Bowyer, the pilot,

immediately ordered "stop engines" and then "full astern", but a collision seemed inevitable. Fortunately, the alert Captain Gale of the tug *Vulcan* swung behind *New York*'s stern and got a wire rope on her port quarter to slow her drift. Danger was averted by no more than a metre or so, and those who had felt ill at ease about coming on the ship must have seen it as another harbinger of bad tidings.

Titanic was now forced to wait an hour while *New York* was taken out of harm's way and additional lines were placed on *Oceanic*. She therefore did not arrive at her first port of call, Cherbourg, until 6:35pm. Cherbourg's piers were not large enough to accommodate *Titanic*, and the two purpose-built White Star tenders, *Nomadic* and *Traffic*, ferried arriving

LEFT: *Passengers excitedly boarding* Titanic *in Southampton, while crew below oversee the embarkation. Many considered it a chance of a lifetime to sail on such a ship.*

THE CREWMEN WHO MISSED THE SHIP

Most of the crew of *Titanic* signed on during Saturday, 6 April. But when the ship sank, 24 of the original crew were not aboard. Of those, ten were listed as "failed to join", eight as deserted and the others as "left by consent", discharged, transferred or "left ship sick". Among the fortunate were the Slade brothers from Southampton – Bertram, Tom and Alfred – each of whom had been signed on as a fireman. They temporarily left the ship for a pint of beer and missed catching it by moments after they were delayed by a slow train in their path.

and departing passengers and cargo from ship to harbour. Twenty-two passengers disembarked, to be replaced by 274, each of whom had made the six-hour train ride from Paris aboard the *Train Transatlantique*. Among these were 47-year-old American mining magnate Benjamin Guggenheim; famed English dress designer Lucy, Lady Duff Gordon and her husband, Sir Cosmo; and Denver socialite Mrs James Brown, known to her friends as "Molly".

An hour and a half later, *Titanic* departed for Queenstown, Ireland, where, at 11am on 11 April, she anchored 3.2 kilometres (two miles) offshore, as once again she was too vast to enter the harbour. White Star tenders took off eight passengers – including Frank Browne, whose

photographs were the last of the ship – and ferried 120 passengers and 1,385 sacks of mail to the ship. Meanwhile, fireman John Coffee stowed away in the offgoing post and disappeared into his native Queenstown. Onboard, an unknown fireman disturbed passengers when his soot-covered face was seen coming out of the hindmost of the ship's four funnels. It was the dummy funnel used as a ventilator rather than a chimney, as the prankster knew full well, but to some of the squeamish aboard, it was an evil omen.

All was now ready for the transatlantic voyage to New York, so at 1:30pm the American flag was raised and those aboard watched the green of Ireland fade into the distance. For many of them, it was the last time they would ever see land.

TOP: *Members of the crew in life jackets. Those who had missed the ship were considered lucky.*

“ We had a very near collision with the American line boat *New York* which delayed us over an hour, & instead of arriving at Cherbourg at 5 o’c we did not get there till 7 o’c & consequently shall be late all through. I am told we shall probably get into New York, provided all goes well, late Tuesday night which means we shall land early Wednesday morning. It is lovely on the water, & except for the smell of new paint, everything is very comfortable on board. **”**

– Marion Wright

TOP: *Frank Browne caught passengers peering out of the windows when it appeared that the suddenly free* New York *(on right) would collide with* Titanic.

ABOVE: *Escorted by tugs,* Titanic *finally gets out into the river test. Already some aboard were disturbed by what they considered evil omens.*

THOMAS HART: DEAD OR ALIVE?

Among the crew officially lost on *Titanic* was a fireman whose discharge book named him as Thomas Hart of 51 College Street, Southampton. So one can imagine his mother's shock when, a month later, her son showed up at the door. It turned out that he had never boarded the ship because the night before joining, he had lost his discharge book in a pub. He was then afraid to admit his story immediately after the disaster. No one has ever determined who signed on in Hart's name – and died for his deception.

TOP: *A picture from a postcard. The luxury liner sits in the dock at Southampton prior to her fatal maiden voyage.*

ABOVE: *The special train for* Titanic *passengers – the first and last, it turned out – waiting to depart Waterloo Station, London, on the morning of 10 April.*

"Anyhow it was exciting when the hawsers began popping one after the other, & the men ran in bunches to escape the flying ends of rope. Now we are running past the Isle of Wight. I hope not to have any more accidents. The ship is like a palace. There is an uninterrupted deck run of 165 yards for exercise and a ripping swimming bath, gymnasium and squash racket court & huge lounge & surrounding verandahs. My cabin is ripping, hot and cold water and a very comfy looking bed & plenty of room....

Your loving Dad **"**

– Lawrence Beasley

TOP: *The White Star Line tenders* Ireland *and* America *at Queenstown's deepwater quay fully loaded with arriving passengers going out to the ship.*

ABOVE: Titanic *steams towards Cherbourg, her first port of call on her maiden voyage. Fully lit up at night, she made a marvellous sight.*

❖ ICE AHEAD ❖

For three days after leaving Queenstown, *Titanic* raced across the Atlantic, accompanied by conditions most passengers loved – blue skies, light winds and calm seas. Yet that state of affairs belied the fact that almost all vessels in the North Atlantic shipping lanes were facing problems of a serious nature. In the far north, the winter had been the mildest in three decades, causing many more icebergs than normal to calve off the Greenland ice shelves. A little farther south, however, temperatures had been cold enough so that as the vast fields of ice drifted south, they did not melt as quickly as usual. The result, as shown by reports of ships during the week beginning 7 April, was that an immense band of ice, extending from 46°North to near 41°30'North and from about 46°18' to 40°40'West, was moving slowly southwest. Since *Titanic* was heading towards "the corner" – a point at 42°North, 47°West at which ships usually set a new course, depending on whether they were going to New York, Boston or other locations – she was aiming directly for this ice.

Sunday was normally a special day aboard ship, and the morning of 14 April was like most others, with Captain Smith conducting the Church of England service in the first-class dining saloon, the assistant purser leading another in the second-class saloon and Father Thomas Byles overseeing the Catholic Mass, first in the second-class lounge, then in the third-class areas. But in the wireless room, the domain of Marconi senior wireless operator Jack Phillips and junior operator Harold Bride, a series of messages began to come through that would soon take on unimagined significance.

In the preceding days, at least a dozen messages had arrived from other ships informing *Titanic* of icebergs ahead. At 9am on the 14th, Phillips received another, from Cunard's *Caronia*, reporting icebergs, "growlers" (smaller but still dangerous pieces of ice) and an extensive field of ice at 42°North, 49–51°West. Phillips immediately took it to Captain Smith, who had it posted on the bridge for his officers. Ice warnings continued to arrive, including some from the Dutch *Noordam* at 11:40am and then, at 1:42pm, from the Greek steamship *Athinai* via White Star's *Baltic*, a message that, rather than post on the bridge, Smith strangely handed to Ismay, who put it in his pocket. Almost simultaneously, another report of ice – at 41°27'North, 50°8'West – was received by Phillips from the German ship *Amerika*, but the chief wireless man, according to Bride, failed to notify any officers.

All told, seven ice warnings were received during the day. One, at 7:30pm, came from the Leyland ship *Californian*, which reported three large icebergs a short distance north of *Titanic's* route. Bride took it to the bridge, but the message did not reach the captain because he was in the à la carte restaurant at a dinner party given in his honour by the wealthy George and Eleanor Widener of Philadelphia. Yet another message, which confirmed heavy pack ice and icebergs, came at 9:40pm from *Mesaba*, but because Bride was sleeping, Phillips was unable to leave his post to take it to the bridge. Meanwhile, the temperature outside began to drop, decreasing from 6.1°C (43°F) at 7pm to 0.5°C (33°F) two hours later.

BOTTOM RIGHT: *Passengers stroll around the second-class boat deck while at anchor off Queenstown, unaware of the terrible conditions they were sailing into.*

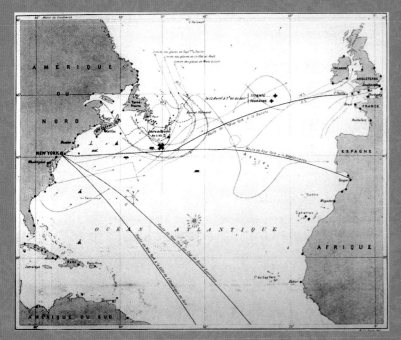

SECOND OFFICER CHARLES LIGHTOLLER

One of the key figures in the chaotic last hours of *Titanic* was 38-year-old Second Officer Charles Lightoller, who had also commanded the last four-hour watch (6–10pm) prior to the collision. Lightoller had gone to sea at 13, joined White Star Line in 1900 and been promoted to first officer before being temporarily dropped back to second officer when Chief Officer Henry Wilde joined *Titanic* late. Throughout the evening, Lightoller expressed concerns about the falling temperature and urged his lookouts to keep their eyes peeled for icebergs despite a calm sea that made spotting them exceptionally difficult.

TOP LEFT: *A French pilot chart showing the intended voyage of* Titanic *across the Atlantic Ocean. Most of the cruise went just as planned, but not all.*

66 I was on watch on the poop in the First Watch (8PM till midnight) on the night of April 14, 1912. The night was pitch black, very calm and starry, around about 11pm I noticed that the weather was becoming colder and [there were] very minute splinters of ice like myriads of coloured lights… [A]bout 11:40pm I was struck by a curious movement of the ship it was similar to going alongside a dock wall rather heavy… as we passed by it I saw it was an iceberg. **99**

– George J Rowe, quatermaster on board Titanic

The final ice warning – as it turned out, *Titanic's* last chance – was sent out at 11pm by Cyril Evans of *Californian*. But the message was not taken by Phillips, who was busy sending and receiving passengers' messages via the Cape Race station in Newfoundland, a task normally carried out at night, when the wireless transmitting range trebled from 650 kilometres (400 miles) during the day to 1,950 kilometres (1,200 miles) at night. Thus, for a variety of reasons, only one of the messages had reached both the captain and the bridge in a timely fashion. In a time of desperate danger, the officers on watch were unaware of the extent of the peril into which they were steaming.

ABOVE: *An illustration from a White Star Line brochure of the second-class boat deck. It is rather ironic that the illustration gives significant attention to the lifeboats.*

CALIFORNIAN ON THE AIR

As well as monitoring traffic for general messages and specific warnings, wireless officers sent and received messages for passengers. At 11pm on 14 April, Jack Phillips was in contact with Cape Race station, when a message burst in from a nearby ship. "Say, old man, we are stopped and surrounded by ice", transmitted Cyril Evans from *Californian*. But before Evans could give his location, Phillips heatedly responded, "Shut up! Shut up! I am busy. I am working Cape Race." Evans, hoping to pass on important information, monitored *Titanic* for 25 minutes, but since *Phillips* continued to transmit, he finally shut down and went to bed.

❝ [I]t was 11:25pm, 14th April when there was a heavy thud and grinding tearing sound. The telegraph in each section signalled down Stop. We had a full head of steam and were doing about 23 knots per hour… We had orders to 'box up' all boilers and put on dampeners to stop steam rising and lifting safety valves. Well, the trimmer came back… and he said 'Blimme we've struck an iceberg'. We thought that a joke. ❞

— George Kemish,
assistant in No.5 Boiler Room

❝ I was on deck in the afternoon of April 14 between 5–6 o'clock and Mr Ismay came and… thrust a Marconigram at me, saying, we were among the icebergs. Something was said about speed and he said that the ship had not been going fast now that they were to start up extra boilers. The telegram also spoke of the *Deutschland*, a ship out of coal and asking for a tow and when I asked him what we were going to do about that he said they had no time for such matters, our ship wanted to do her best and something was said about getting in Tuesday night. ❞

— Emily Borie Ryerson

ABOVE LEFT: *Jack Phillips, the senior wireless operator, had celebrated his 25th birthday aboard* Titanic. *His dedication to the passengers' messages prevented him from receiving a key ice warning.*

ABOVE RIGHT: *An illustration from the time of the miles-long ice field that lay in the path of* Titanic, *including a series of icebergs, one of which dealt the death blow to the ship.*

❖ THE COLLISION ❖

Despite the repeated warnings of ice throughout the day, by 11:30pm on 14 April, *Titanic* was still racing along at nearly 22 knots. The ship was well supplied with specialist lookouts, and in such clear conditions, Captain Smith assumed any ice would be seen far ahead. However, not only was the night moonless, thereby eliminating the sheen off the surface of any ice, but the conditions were so calm, with no waves and no breeze, that normal wave action, which would form a lighter ring around the base of any icebergs, was absent.

About 15 metres (50 feet) above the forecastle deck, lookouts Fred Fleet and Reginald Lee stared out of the crow's nest into the darkness. At 11:30pm they spied a misty haze on the horizon but could not make out anything definite, in part because the binoculars for the lookouts had disappeared before the ship reached Queenstown. They could only strain with the naked eye to see through the darkness.

Suddenly, at 11:40pm, Fleet spotted a dark object dead ahead. He immediately rang the 41-centimetre (16-inch) brass bell that hung above him and picked up the phone to the bridge, which was answered by Sixth Officer James Moody. "Iceberg right ahead", Fleet stated. Within moments, First Officer William Murdoch ordered "Hard a-starboard" (dictating that the ship's bow would swing to port), telegraphed the engine room "Stop. Full speed astern" and closed the ship's watertight doors.

Titanic began to swing to port away from the iceberg – one point, then two – but it was not enough. The iceberg had been spotted at less than 450 metres (500 yards), and although the top of the ship did not collide with it, deep below the waterline some 90 metres (300 feet) of the hull scraped and bumped against the ice. The intense pressure caused the plates to buckle and the rivets to pop, opening a long, intermittent gash that penetrated the first five compartments, including the forward boiler room.

ABOVE: *First Officer William Murdoch, who did not survive the tragedy. Although he has been portrayed negatively at times, there is no evidence that his behaviour was anything but proper throughout the events.*

“ When we were clean of the ship I said what's the best thing to do Mr Ismay he replied you're in charge we could see nothing only this white light so I told them to pull away. Mr Ismay on one oar Mr Carter on another and the 4 of the crew one each and one I steered with 7 oars. We had been pulling for about 10 minutes when we heard a noise like an immense heap of gravel being tipped from a height then she disappeared. We pulled on but seemed to make no headway gradually dawn came and soon we could make out some boats and more ice. ”

– George R. Rowe

“ Mr Phillips now told me that apparently we had struck something, as previous to my turning out he had felt the ship tremble and stop, and expressed an opinion that we should have to return to Belfast. I took over the Telephone from him and he was preparing to retire when Captain Smith entered the cabin and told us to get assistance immediately. Mr Phillips then resumed the phones, after asking the Captain if he should use the regulation distress call CQD. The Captain said 'Yes' and Mr Phillips started in with CQD, having obtained the Latitude and Longitude of the Titanic. ”

– Harold Bride

ABOVE: *Although this picture was taken hours later, after the sun rose, this is thought to be the iceberg with which* Titanic *collided. Some passengers claimed they saw streaks of paint on it.*

THE ILLUSTRATED LONDON NEWS

REGISTERED AS A NEWSPAPER FOR TRANSMISSION IN THE UNITED KINGDOM, AND TO CANADA AND NEWFOUNDLAND BY MAGAZINE POST.

No. 3809. - VOL. CXL   SATURDAY, APRIL 20. 1912.   SIXPENCE.

The Copyright of all the Editorial Matter, both Engravings and Letterpress, is Strictly Reserved in Great Britain, the Colonies, Europe, and the United States of America.

NORTH ATLANTIC ICEBERGS

It is likely that the iceberg with which *Titanic* collided calved from a major glacier in West Greenland. Each year, some 10,000–15,000 large icebergs or smaller chunks of ice known as "growlers" float south to the region in which *Titanic* sank. Icebergs are composed of fresh water, with approximately seven-eighths of their mass below the water line; mass does not refer to height out of the water, which can vary greatly in proportion. The iceberg that *Titanic* hit was estimated to be 15–30 metres (50–100 feet) high above the water and 60–120 metres (200–400 feet) long.

Within a minute, Captain Smith had raced to the bridge, and he quickly sent Fourth Officer Joseph Boxhall to ascertain the extent of the damage. Most of the passengers were not aware of the severity of the impact, although some were intrigued that large fragments of ice had come cascading down on the forward well deck, while others claimed to have felt anything from a slight shock or trembling to a strong jar accompanied by a grinding noise.

It was considerably worse than that in boiler room No. 6, where Second Engineer James Hesketh and Frederick Barrett, a leading stoker, heard a terrible rending sound and water suddenly exploded through a gash about 60 centimetres (2 feet) above the floor. They dived into the next room as the watertight door closed, only to find another tear in the steel plates and another jet of water shooting towards them. By the time they climbed to a higher deck, the water in No. 6 boiler room had already risen 2.4 metres (8 feet).

Within 15 minutes, Boxhall reported back to Captain Smith, who shortly thereafter received an even grimmer report from Thomas Andrews of Harland & Wolff. Andrews had quickly realized the gravity of the situation. *Titanic* could float with any two of her watertight compartments flooded; she could even remain afloat if it were the first four compartments that were breached. But five had been opened up, and the fifth – boiler room No. 6 – and those after it did not have watertight bulkheads that extended to the uppermost decks. When boiler room No. 6 finished flooding, the water still pouring in would reach E deck, and would then overflow into the sixth "watertight" compartment from above. As each successive compartment filled and the bow was pulled further under, the next compartment would again start to fill.

Andrews informed Smith that the "unsinkable" ship was going to do just that. No one knew better than Andrews that they were far short of the necessary lifeboats, meaning many of the passengers, like *Titanic* herself, had only an hour or two to live.

ABOVE: *This photo of an iceberg was the main feature of page one of* The Illustrated London News *on 20 April 1912, when the weekly paper carried the story of the sinking of* Titanic.

THOMAS ANDREWS

No one knew *Titanic* better than 39-year-old Thomas Andrews, managing director for Harland & Wolff in charge of design. Andrews joined the company at the age of 16 as an apprentice and eventually rose to a position of prominence. He boarded *Titanic* in Belfast to determine if any adjustments were needed, and to oversee the company's "Guarantee Group" that would effect the changes. After advising Captain Smith that the ship was doomed, he encouraged passengers to make their way to the lifeboats. He was last seen in the first-class smoking room, staring into space with his life-jacket in front of him.

❝ I was a bride of 50 days. My husband and I were on our way to America to make it our home. He had been to America before where he had a business. When I first realized that something was wrong, it was 11 o'clock at night and I was fast asleep. Suddenly I heard a tremendous noise and immediately I knew the ship had been hit hard. It almost threw me off the bed. The motor stopped at once. My husband and I jumped up and ran to see what had happened. We went to the engine room and saw the crew trying to repair parts of the ship. We were still wearing our nightclothes. **❞**

– Celiney Decker

ABOVE LEFT: *Thomas Andrews helped many passengers to safety when he knew the ship was doomed.*

ABOVE RIGHT: *This evocative picture from France's* Le Petit Journal *does not show the way* Titanic *actually struck the iceberg, but it got its message across to its readers.*

TELEGRAM.

The White House,

Washington.

8 WU. S. FD. 100 Paid Day Letter 11:00 a.m.

Wilmington, N.C., April 19, 1912.

Wm. H. Taft,
    Washington, D.C.

    Thousands of Southerns have been hoping with you that news today would
in some way herald the safety of Major Butt, although fully realizing that
the chivalry of his nature would admit of no compromise until the women and
children were safe, realizing the depth of your own nature and feeling our
sympathy has gone out to you in the past four days of severe ordeal and we
feel satisfied you will brook no compromise in the matter of adopting measure
which will forestall and prevent the recurrence of the horrible fatality which
befell the passengers of the ill-fated TITANIC.

                                        Chas. N. Evans.

❖ CONDOLENCE TELEGRAM ❖

ABOVE: A telegram of 19 April 1912 from Charles N Evans to
President William H Taft, expressing sympathy of "Thousands
of Southerners" about the fate of Major Butt, and hope that
measures will be adopted to prevent further such accidents.

❧ CROSS SECTION ❧

BELOW: A cross section of *Titanic* showing the impact of the collision with the iceberg.

THE BUCKLED PLATES

BILGE KEEL

FIRST CLASS STATE ROOMS

POST MAIL ROOM

DOUBLE BOTTOM

KEEL

ICE PENETRATING THE DOUBLE BOTTOM

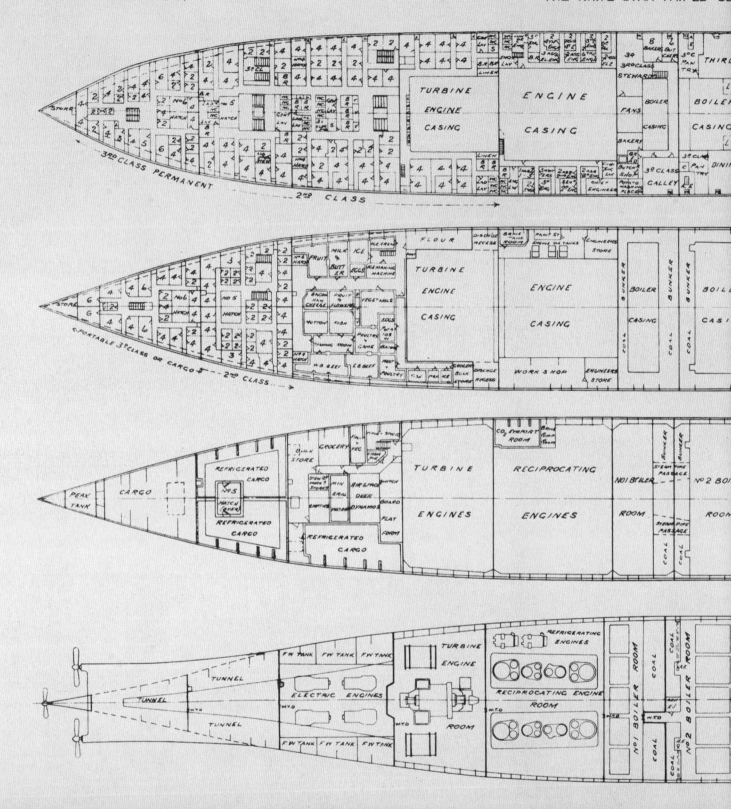

BLUEPRINT

ABOVE: A blueprint showing the deck section of *Titanic*.

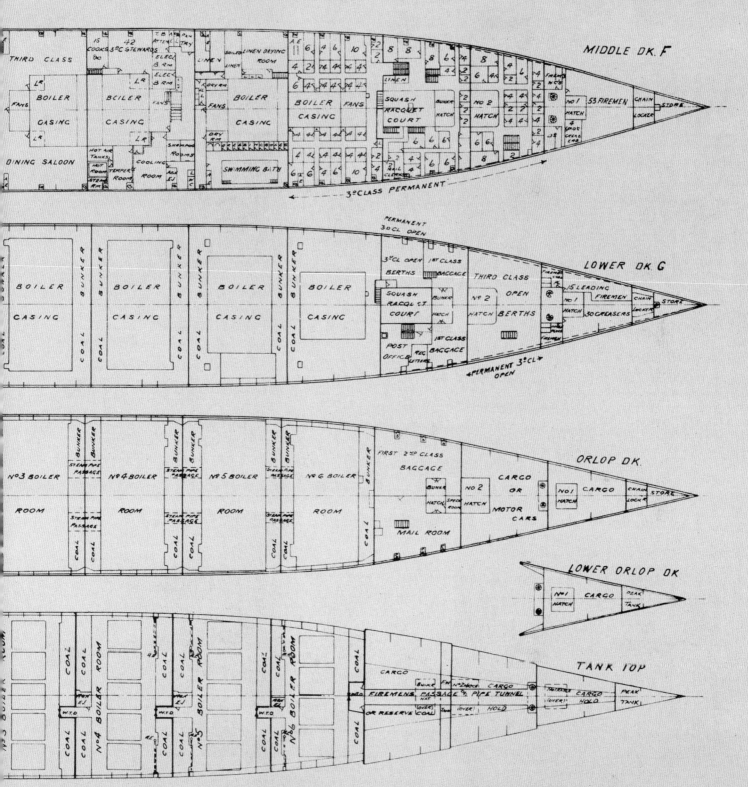

SINKING SKETCH

RIGHT: A detailed sketch of the sinking of *Titanic* produced by a survivor, John B Thayer.

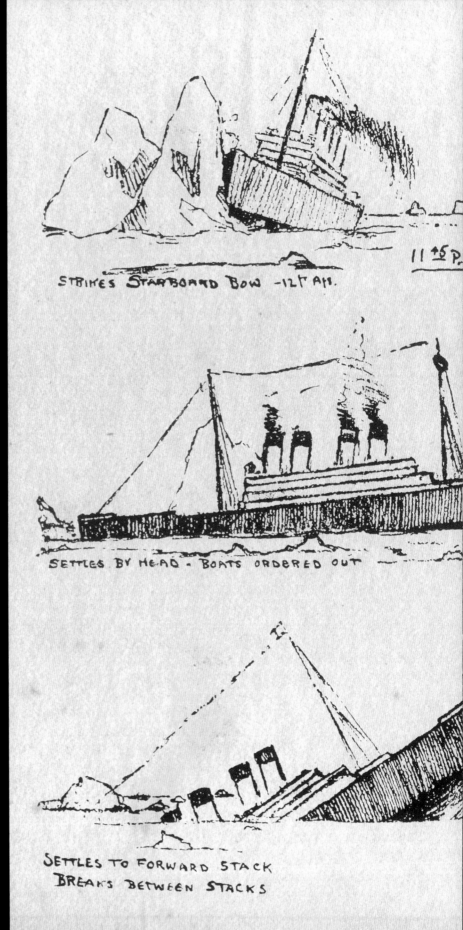

FORWARD END FLOATS,
THEN SINKS.

1.50 AM.

12:05 AM

STERN SECTION
PIVOTS AMIDSHIPS AND
SWINGS OVER SPOT WHERE FORWARD SECTION SANK.

2:00 AM.

1.40 AM

LAST POSITION
IN WHICH "Titanic"
STAYED 5 MINUTES BEFORE
THE FINAL PLUNGE.

L.P. Skidmore,
S.S. "Carpathia" Apr. 15th
1912.

MAN THE LIFEBOATS

As soon as it became obvious that *Titanic* was mortally wounded, Captain Smith ordered the crew to be mustered, the lifeboats to be uncovered and the passengers brought up to the decks. He then directed Fourth Officer Joseph Boxhall to calculate the ship's position. His estimate – 41°46'North, 50°14'West, which was off by many miles – was taken to Jack Phillips in the wireless room, who began sending out distress calls.

The inefficiency and confusion brought about by sailing on what was perceived as an "unsinkable" ship quickly became apparent. There was not a consistent plan of action, most of the crew had not received adequate training in launching the lifeboats and the captain had not held the standard passenger lifeboat drill. Moreover, most of the passengers were already in their cabins, there was no public address system and when the stewards informed the passengers of the situation, they gave widely varying instructions. Slowly, however, a number of people made their way to the promenades and boat decks.

At 12:25am, Smith ordered the loading of lifeboats, with women and children first. Even this was carried out haphazardly as, on port side, men were denied access to the boats, while on starboard they were allowed in if there were no women waiting. The actual loading of the boats began to bring home the reality of the dangers, and many passengers crowded the pursers' offices to demand their valuables back.

Several other problems became apparent as the boats were loaded. First, many of the passengers were extremely hesitant and, after looking at the water far below, chose to not leave the comforts of the ship for the tiny, creaking vessels. In addition, the officers were concerned about loading the boats too heavily, evidently unaware that the new Welin davits were able to withstand the full load of 65 adults. One plan was to lower the boats half-full, and then take more passengers from the gangway doors at water level, but the men sent to open the doors disappeared. Boat after boat went down the side with numerous empty spaces on it.

At about 12:45am, First Officer William Murdoch ordered the first lifeboat – Number 7 on the starboard side – to be lowered away with only 28 people aboard. Near the same time, Boxhall fired off the first of a series of distress rockets. Hope increased when the lights of another ship became visible some 10–16 kilometres (6–10 miles) off the port side.

Lifeboat 5 was the second boat lowered, with some 40 occupants. In command of it was Third Officer Herbert Pittman, whom Murdoch sent so that he could also look after the other boats when they reached the water. Also in the boat was Quartermaster Alfred Olliver, who, as it descended, desperately tried to find the plug for

❝ I had not heard the Band Playing, but in the distance I could hear people singing 'For Those in Peril on the Sea'. After a while Mr Webb got all the Lifeboats to keep together as he said there was a better chance to be seen. We transferred our 58 passengers to the other boats, and then started to search for any survivors after the ship had disappeared. Before she sank we could see her well down at the Fore port and her stern well out of the water. Some lights were still showing and continued to do so till she took the final plunge. ❞

– A. Pugh

BOTTOM RIGHT: *The life-jacket worn by Madeleine Astor. It is now part of the* Titanic *Historical Society Collection held at the* Titanic *Museum in Indian Orchard, Massachusetts.*

CQD: THE WIRELESS EFFORTS

At 12:15am, Jack Phillips started tapping out the emergency signal "CQD" (often said to stand for "Come Quick, Danger"), followed by *Titanic's* call letters – MGY – and her estimated position. Ten minutes later, Harold Cottam of *Carpathia*, 94 kilometres (58 miles) away, came onto the frequency to tell Phillips there were numerous messages from Cape Cod for *Titanic*. Receiving Phillips' distress signal, the amazed Cottam responded, "Shall I tell my captain? Do you require assistance?" "Yes", Phillips replied. "Come quick." Cottam raced to the bridge, Captain Arthur Rostron was awoken, and within minutes *Carpathia* was on her way.

the hole through which excess water drained when the boat was stored. Confronted by uncooperative passengers, he succeeded in finding and inserting the plug only after the boat had reached the sea and started taking water.

Meanwhile, on the port side, some 25 women were loaded into Lifeboat 6, with Quartermaster Robert Hichens and lookout Frederick Fleet, who had first seen the iceberg, as the only crew. Second Officer Charles Lightoller ordered Hichens to row the vessel to the ship in the distance and come back for more passengers. As the boat started to descend, Mrs Margaret "Molly" Brown of Denver – who had just persuaded several fearful women to get in and was going to help out elsewhere – was grabbed by two well meaning acquaintances and dropped 1.2 metres (four feet) over the side into the boat. She quickly realized there were not enough men to row to the distant light and demanded more. With Lightoller's blessing, Major Arthur Peuchen, a Canadian yachtsman, swung out 1.8 metres (6 feet) onto the ropes and let himself down hand-over-hand.

As more boats reached the water below, the anxious people still aboard *Titanic* began to realize that many of them were not going to survive.

TOP: *This, the only known picture of the wireless office aboard* Titanic, *was taken by Father Browne on his short stay aboard the ship. Jack Phillips spent his last hours desperately signalling for help from here.*

DOG THE LIFEBOATS

Just as every other whim of *Titanic*'s first-class passengers was catered to, dog owners were pleased by spotless kennels and crew detailed to walk the dogs daily. There were so many dogs aboard that a show had even been scheduled. Although honeymooning Helen Bishop had insisted her dog Frou Frou reside in her cabin, she left it behind because she acknowledged there was not enough room for all the people. Two dogs did survive, however. Margaret Hays took her Pomeranian into Lifeboat 7, and Henry Harper escaped in Lifeboat 3 with his Pekinese named Sun Yat Sen.

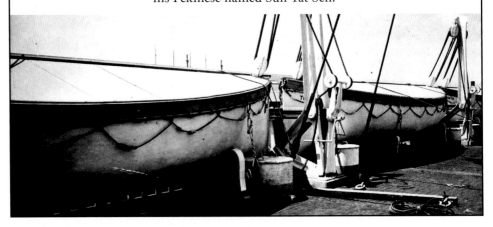

TOP: *This well known painting shows the bravery, the anguish and the fear shown by passengers and crew alike as the women and children were loaded into the lifeboats.*

ABOVE LEFT: *Major Arthur Peuchen, the yachtsman who volunteered to help row Lifeboat 16. He survived, but suffering the stigma of having been a man in one of the lifeboats for the rest of his life.*

ABOVE RIGHT: *A low-level view of the lifeboats aboard* Titanic, *as the dogs aboard would have seen them. The dogs were less fortunate regarding the lifeboats than even the human passengers were.*

"All the boats were gone by now except No 9 and there was a bit of Trouble there the Chief officer was threatening someone and fired 2 revolver shots shouting now will you get back I was not near enough to see if anyone was shot after No 9 had left the Chief Officer shouted any crew here and about 7–8 stepped forward and he said hurry men up there and put that boat adrift it was a collapsible on Top of the Smokeroom we got it down to the deck but could not overhaul boats fall [sic] as they were hanging down shipside in water."

– Walter Hurst

"The Boat Deck was thronged with people. Many women and children had to be forcibly put in the Boats. They felt much more safe on the Decks of the Big Liner than in the small boats about 90 FT above the water line. Therefore the Boats that got away first did not take half the number of people they could have done, and then later when we realized things were really serious the boats getting away later were very much overloaded. The Band had stopped playing by now, about the last person I took particular notice of was W.T. Stead (novelist) calmly reading in the First Class Smoke room."

– George Kemish

↓ 75 FEET FROM BOAT DECK TO WATER.

ABOVE: *An illustration of a lifeboat being lowered down the side of* Titanic *shows how far the boats had to descend to the water and why some passengers were concerned about entering them.*

NEXT PAGE: *A stunning painting of* Titanic *at night by renowned* Titanic *artist Ken Marschall.*

THE BAND PLAYS ON

While *Titanic's* bows dipped deeper into the water, and the lifeboat operation proceeded, passengers and crew responded to the emergency in many different ways. Some passengers steadfastly remained in their cabins, refusing to believe there was an emergency. Others, such as 21-year-old tennis star R Norris Williams – who was travelling to the US prior to entering Harvard – stoically wandered the ship, unwilling to enter a lifeboat when women and children were still aboard. At one point, Norris and his father found a steward unable to open the door to a first-class cabin, in which a woman was beginning to panic. Williams dropped his shoulder and broke the door in, prompting the steward to announce that he would have to report him for damaging company property.

Upstairs, several members of Wallace Hartley's eight-man orchestra began playing in the first-class lounge to help relieve the tension. The other members soon joined them and eventually, as the passengers headed outside, the band followed them to the boat deck. Legend has it that the bandsmen remained at their instruments until the very end.

Meanwhile, members of the crew desperately struggled to minimize the disaster. Fourth Officer Joseph Boxhall was joined by Quartermaster George Rowe in firing off distress rockets at five-minute intervals. By means of a Morse lamp, they also tried to contact the unknown ship, which was so close that they could make out her red and green sidelights. Despite their best efforts, after about an hour the mysterious ship vanished into the night. Throughout the same period, all 34 engineering officers remained at their posts, maintaining *Titanic*'s lighting and other electrical systems until moments before she sank; every one of them was lost with the ship.

Many passengers also showed remarkable courage in the crisis, and did their utmost to help others. Four men – railway director Charles M Hays, automobile designer Washington Augustus Roebling II, Howard Case and Thornton Davidson – turned down the opportunity to enter Lifeboat 3 and instead assisted numerous

women and children at a variety of boat stations before calmly accepting their fates. Others seemed unconcerned, perhaps because of their fervent belief in *Titanic* being unsinkable. For example, after hearing the call to don life-jackets, Major Archibald Butt, military aide to President William Howard Taft, finished his card game in the first-class smoking room with Clarence Moore, Harry Widener and William Carter before adjourning

BRAVE AS THE "BIRKENHEAD" BAND: THE "TITANIC'S" MUSICIAN HEROES

LEFT: *The funeral for Wallace Hartley on 25 May 1912 in his hometown of Colne, Lancashire, drew thousands from all over the country wishing to pay their last respects.*

ABOVE: *Richard Norris Williams went on to become one of the world's premier tennis players and represented the United States in Davis Cup action numerous times, including as captain.*

> **I was now assisted in pushing off a collapsible lifeboat, which was on the port side of the forward funnel, onto the boat deck. Just as the boat fell, I noticed Captain Smith dive from the bridge into the sea. Then I followed a general scramble down on to the boat deck, but no sooner had we got there than the sea washed over. I managed to catch hold of the boat we had previously fixed up and was swept overboard with her. I then experienced the most exciting three or four hours anyone could reasonably wish for and was in due course, with the rest of the survivors, picked up by the *Carpathia*.**
>
> *– Harold Bride*

THE FINAL NUMBER

There has long been debate over the last music played by *Titanic*'s bandsmen. Major Peuchen claimed he heard "Alexander's Ragtime Band" while in Lifeboat 6. Wireless operator Harold Bride stated that after playing ragtime tunes, the band concluded with the hymn "Autumn". This was not in White Star's music book, however, and it has been suggested that Bride was actually referring to the waltz "Songe d'Automne". Or was it, as numerous survivors claimed, "Nearer My God to Thee"? This was Wallace Hartley's favourite hymn, but it still leaves open the question of which of three tunes the hymn was played to: "Bethany", "Horbury" or "Proprior Deo".

DANGER FROM ABOVE

Shortly before 1:30am, Lifeboat 13 was lowered with 64 people, swaying dangerously as it descended. When it reached the surface, water pouring from the flooded condenser exhaust system pushed it directly beneath Lifeboat 15. The crew tried to release the ropes, but they were so taut the mechanism would not work. The cries of those on Lifeboat 13 were not heard, and Lifeboat 15 continued down until those below could touch its hull. Finally, two crewmen, Fred Barrett and Robert Hopkins, grabbed knives and cut the ropes, narrowly preventing the boat being crushed.

ABOVE LEFT: *Lifeboat 15 threatens to crush lifeboat 13 from above. Had the boat on the water not just escaped, another 64 people would undoubtedly have lost their lives.*

ABOVE RIGHT: *A memorial to the musicians aboard* Titanic. *This was erected in Southampton in 1990 on the same site as one unveiled in 1913 but destroyed during the Second World War.*

to see what was happening. Colonel Archibald Gracie, an American historian, cancelled his planned Monday morning match with the ship's squash professional before making his way to the boat deck.

All the while, lifeboats continued to be loaded haphazardly. At about 1:00am, number 3 went down the side with fewer than 50 people, 15 of them crew. Shortly thereafter, First Officer William Murdoch prepared the first of the two smaller lifeboats, with a capacity of 40. With only a handful of people nearby, rather than call for others, Murdoch had it launched holding only a dozen: five passengers – including Sir Cosmo Duff Gordon and his wife, Lucile – and seven crew.

As the deck of the ship tilted more precariously and the true danger of the situation became increasingly obvious, the officers finally began to load the boats more fully. Around 1:20am, Lifeboat 9 was sent out with 56 people. About 20 minutes later, numbers 11 and 15 had about 70 occupants each – more than the tested limit. As Lifeboat 14 was lowered at 1:30am containing some 60 people (almost all women), Fifth Officer Harold Lowe went with it in order to take charge of the boats on the water. But he was so worried they would be overwhelmed by frightened men that he pulled his revolver to keep them back. The boats were running out, and so was precious time for those aboard *Titanic*.

ABOVE: *The signal lamps being inspected by a port official while* Titanic *was at Queenstown. Tragically, the "Mystery Ship" did not respond to requests for emergency help via the lamps.*

THE RICH, FAMOUS AND UNFORTUNATE

S ince *Titanic* was considered the most luxurious ship in the world, it is not surprising that some of those who died essentially comprised a "who's who'" of the financial, social and artistic worlds.

The wealthiest person aboard was 47-year-old John Jacob Astor IV. The great-grandson and namesake of a man who had earned both fame and enormous fortune first in the fur trade and then in real estate investments in New York City, Astor had taken over the management of his family's New York properties while still in his mid-twenties. He made large sums from owning overcrowded and run-down tenements that were rented to immigrants, but he also profited from building offices, apartment buildings and hotels. In 1897, he financed the Astoria Hotel adjoining his cousin's Waldorf Hotel, and the new complex became world-famous as the Waldorf-Astoria. Astor also wrote science fiction, invented mechanical devices and served in the military long enough to reach the rank of colonel.

Another prominent military figure aboard *Titanic* was Major Archibald Butt. He was originally a journalist, through which he gained many contacts in Washington, leading in turn to him being appointed as first secretary of the American Embassy in Mexico. In 1898, during the Spanish–American War, he joined the army as a lieutenant. In the next eight years, he served in the Philippines and Cuba before becoming a military aid to President Theodore Roosevelt and then to his successor, William Howard Taft. Suffering ill health in early 1912, Butt holidayed in Europe for six weeks – travelling for part of it with the artist Francis Millet – before the two boarded *Titanic*.

Like Astor, 50-year-old George Widener came from a wealthy background. His father had been a founding partner of the hugely successful Philadelphia Traction Company and was on the board of Fidelity Trust, the bank that controlled

IMMC, owner of the White Star Line. The younger Widener eventually took charge of the Philadelphia Traction Company and oversaw the development of lucrative cable and electric streetcar operations. A patron of the arts, he lived at Lynnewood Hall, a 110-room French classical-style mansion outside Philadelphia. Although Widener's wife, Eleanor, survived, Widener and their 27-year-old son, Harry, did not.

Like Madeleine Astor and Eleanor Widener, Pennsylvania steel millionaire Arthur Ryerson's wife Emily boarded Lifeboat 4, and like the others, she lost her husband. The Ryersons had been visiting Europe when they learned of the accidental death of their son, Arthur Jr. Wishing to hurry home, they booked passage on *Titanic*. Unbeknown to them, a distant cousin, William E Ryerson, was also aboard as a dining saloon steward; he survived the tragedy.

ABOVE: *Major Archibald Butt began his career in journalism as a reporter for the* Louiseville Courier-Journal. *While an officer in the US army, he served in the Philippines and Cuba.*

66 When she struck at a quarter to twelve and the engines stopped I knew very well something was wrong. Doctor Simpson came and told me the mails were afloat. I knew things were pretty bad. He brought Miss Marsden and I into his room and gave us a little whisky and water. I laughed and asked him if he thought we needed it, and he said we should. Miss Marsden was crying, he was cross with her. He asked me if I was afraid, I replied I was not. He said well spoken like a true Ulster girl. He had to hurry away to see if anyone was hurt. We helped him on with his greatcoat, I never saw him again. 99

– Mary Sloan

ASTOR AT THE DISASTER

In 1909, Astor divorced his wife of 18 years, and two years later he married Madeleine Force, who, at 18, was two years younger than his son. Gossip about the respectability of the union led the couple to spend the winter abroad, hoping the scandal would die down in their absence. They joined *Titanic* at Cherbourg. On the night of the disaster, Astor helped Madeleine, who was five months pregnant, into Lifeboat 4 and then asked to accompany her. After being told that only women and children would be admitted, he calmly stepped back and waved goodbye.

ABOVE LEFT: *John Jacob Astor and his wife Madeleine. She escaped in Lifeboat 4 and in August gave birth to John Jacob Astor V. She relinquished any claim to the Astor fortune when she married William Dick in 1916.*

ABOVE RIGHT: *The original Waldorf-Astoria Complex. The Waldorf Hotel opened in 1893 and the Astoria Hotel four years later. Today, this site is occupied by the Empire State Building.*

Meanwhile, Ida Straus, the wife of another wealthy passenger, was unwilling to leave her husband. Isidor Straus had emigrated with his family from Bavaria at the age of nine in 1854, and through years of work had built a mercantile empire, eventually acquiring ownership with his brother of Macy's department store in New York. He also had once been elected to Congress. Now, after the collision, Ida started to get into Lifeboat 8, but she changed her mind and returned to her husband. Others nearby appealed to Straus to enter the boat, stating that no one would mind him doing so, but he refused to get in as long as there were still women and children aboard the sinking ship. The couple left the deck to share their final moments, while the lifeboat was sent out less than half-full, as so many of them were.

Throughout the night, other influential men – including Charles M Hayes, the president of Canada's Grand Trunk Pacific Railroad, American short-story writer Jacques Futrelle and Christopher Head, a former mayor of Chelsea – showed remarkable poise. Few displayed more panache, however, than American mining magnate Benjamin Guggenheim. When the futility of the situation became apparent, he and his valet Victor Giglio disappeared below. Returning in full evening dress, Guggenheim announced: "We've dressed up in our best and are prepared to go down like gentlemen."

TOP LEFT: *Isidor and Ida Straus. In the years immediately following the disaster, their decision to stay with each other aboard made them perhaps the most revered of all* Titanic *passengers.*

ABOVE LEFT: *Christopher Head had entered his father's London firm of naval underwriters at the age of 36. He later served as mayor of Chelsea, and was travelling to the US on business on* Titanic.

TOP RIGHT: *Benjamin Guggenheim was the fifth of seven sons of the incredibly wealthy mining magnate Meyer Guggenheim, allowing him to lead a life of luxury and leisure.*

❝Although it is only a little over four weeks since the *Titanic* struck it seems as many months or years to me. You can well understand the awful dread and anxiety of the first week when, day and night, we haunted the offices of the White Star Line and the Associated Press, hoping always to find a name that never appeared among the survivors. At first, when we thought that nearly all were saved and the *Carpathia* was bound for Halifax, Vincent and I arranged to go to Halifax, and we changed our plan only one hour before the train left, as we found the *Carpathia* was coming direct to New York. Then followed days of suspense...**❞**

– W.H. Dobyn

THE SAGA OF LIFEBOAT 4

One of the first lifeboats to be readied was Lifeboat 4, which at 12:30am was swung out and lowered one level so that it was next to the promenade deck. There, a group of well-heeled passengers – the Astors, Wideners, Ryersons, Thayers and Carters – had been assembled. However, no one could open the windows in the canopy surrounding the deck, and after half an hour the group was shuttled up to the boat deck. But now there was no one to haul the lifeboat back up again, so, after another lengthy wait, they once again traipsed down to the promenade deck. There the windows were finally opened, and the women and children were able to enter the lifeboat. Despite there being only about 35 people in the boat, husbands were not allowed to enter it, and at about 1:55am it was finally lowered, one of the last boats to leave the ship.

ABOVE: *The first-class dining saloon of* Titanic *spread majestically across the entire width of the ship. Measuring 92 x 114 feet (28 x 35 metres), it was described in* The Shipbuilder *as "by far the largest room afloat."*

❧ W T STEAD ❧

Although a number of people who lost their lives on *Titanic* have been remembered because they were extremely wealthy or socially prominent, perhaps the passenger best known and most widely respected at the time was the renowned English journalist and spiritualist William Thomas Stead.

Born in Northumberland in 1849, the son of a Congregationalist minister, Stead found his calling when he began writing for Darlington's *Northern Echo*, of which he became editor in 1871. In short order, he made it one of the loudest advocates for social reform in the country, supporting the Liberal Party, women's suffrage, compulsory universal education, collective bargaining and Irish home rule. His support of Gladstone was so strong that the Prime Minister urged John Morley, who was editor of *The Pall*

Mall Gazette of London, to hire Stead as the assistant editor for this small but very powerful Liberal evening newspaper.

Stead joined *The Pall Mall Gazette* in 1880, succeeding Morley three years later when the latter entered Parliament. For the next seven years, Stead tried to prove that the press could shape and voice the desires and opinions of an increasingly literate British electorate, and that public opinion via the press could determine government policy. The first step in fulfilling this mission was to make his newspaper stand out, and to do so he introduced American-style sensationalism to the British press. His innovations included using bold headlines, crossheads to break up the text, political cartoons and maps, diagrams and other pictorial illustrations. Eschewing traditional anonymous journalism, he also developed the signed leader (or editorial), book reviews and drama criticism and special interviews – all of which led the famed scholar-poet Matthew Arnold to coin the pejorative term "New Journalism" for Stead's innovative techniques. Stead's most famous interview was with General Charles Gordon, and his demand afterwards to send Gordon to the Sudan to relieve Anglo-Egyptian garrisons sparked a campaign that put so much pressure on Gladstone that the government grudgingly dispatched Gordon to Khartoum. Gordon met his death there in 1885.

Of all of Stead's contributions, however, his greatest were his investigative crusades, through which he tried to open the eyes of the British public and government to moral, political and economic injustices. These included the "Bitter

ABOVE: *Stead with his wife Emma and their six children in 1891. Stead lived in Wimbledon Park and took the train into London each day while editor of* The Pall Mall Gazette.

"MAIDEN TRIBUTE OF MODERN BABYLON"

Stead's greatest crusade was known as the "Maiden Tribute of Modern Babylon". In an effort to compel Parliament to raise the age of consent for girls from 13 to 16, Stead personally conducted an investigation into the sale and trade of children for sexual purposes, the results of which he published in shocking detail in July 1885. The ensuing uproar forced the enactment of the Criminal Law Amendment Bill restricting child prostitution. Owing to a technical violation in procuring his information – but actually because he had embarrassed so many powerful people – Stead was sentenced to a three-month prison term.

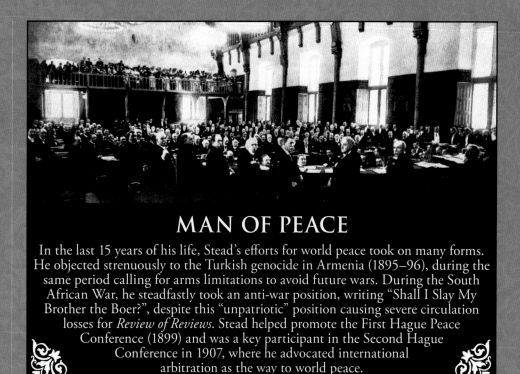

MAN OF PEACE

In the last 15 years of his life, Stead's efforts for world peace took on many forms. He objected strenuously to the Turkish genocide in Armenia (1895–96), during the same period calling for arms limitations to avoid future wars. During the South African War, he steadfastly took an anti-war position, writing "Shall I Slay My Brother the Boer?", despite this "unpatriotic" position causing severe circulation losses for *Review of Reviews*. Stead helped promote the First Hague Peace Conference (1899) and was a key participant in the Second Hague Conference in 1907, where he advocated international arbitration as the way to world peace.

to leave it in 1890 to become editor (and soon owner) of the monthly *Review of Reviews*. For the next two decades, this served as his platform to advocate the union of English-speaking peoples, the confederation of the Empire, the success of the temperance and suffragist movements, the improvement of Anglo–American and Anglo–Russian relations and morality and honesty in politics.

In Stead's later years, much of his energy went in two directions. He was a firm believer in psychic phenomena, and for several years produced a quarterly about it entitled *Borderland*. He also published some of his own experiences with "automatic writing" – said to be a way to receive communications from the spirit world – in a book entitled *Letters from Julia*. Stead's other active involvement late in life was the advancement of world peace. So high was the regard with which he was held in this cause that he was invited by American President William Howard Taft to speak on international peace at the Great Men and Religions Conference in New York.

Stead sailed on *Titanic* in order to attend the conference. In the ship's final hour, he was seen escorting women and children from third-class to the boat deck.

Cry of Outcast London" campaign, attacking the problems of London's slums; the "Truth About the Navy" campaign, which helped lead to the enlargement and modernization of the Royal Navy and his ongoing condemnation of government – and particularly police – violations of free speech and other civil liberties following "Bloody Sunday" in Trafalgar Square. Disagreements with the proprietor of *The Pall Mall Gazette* led Stead

ABOVE: *Stead in the uniform assigned to him in Holloway Prison. He actually gloried in having been incarcerated for noble reasons and donned the uniform annually on the anniversary of his imprisonment.*

TOP RIGHT: *The delegates in the main conference room of the Second Hague Peace Conference. Like the first conference, which was initiated by Tsar Nicolas II of Russia, this conference was hosted by The Netherlands.*

ABOVE RIGHT: *Stead in Constantinople in October 1911. He was highly critical of the Turkish regime and its genocide against the Armenians. This was one of his last trips before his death.*

THE SHIP SINKS

As the front end of the ship sank deeper, among the last hopes for survival were the four collapsible boats. These had canvas sides that could be raised and held up by stanchions, but on a normal basis could be stored flat. Collapsible C was loaded to two-thirds capacity before a group of men appeared ready to rush it around 1:45am. Chief Purser Herbert McElroy stopped them by firing his revolver twice. Just as it began to be lowered, two other men quietly sneaked into it. They were William Carter, who had been refused entry into Lifeboat 4 with his family, and J Bruce Ismay of White Star.

At 2:05am, Collapsible D was the last boat launched, when Chief Officer Henry Wilde sent it out only half-full because, with the water rapidly rising, he believed it might not otherwise get off at all. As it began to be lowered, Second Officer Charles Lightoller drew his pistol and ordered several crewmen to form a barrier to prevent it from being overwhelmed by a surge of men arriving from the lower decks. Wilde instructed Lightoller to get in the boat, but the Second Officer refused to leave his post. Meanwhile, as Collapsible D dropped past them on the promenade deck, two first-class passengers – Hugh Woolmer and Mauritz Björnstrom-Steffansson – seeing the water lapping the deck, leapt together into the boat.

Lightoller was not alone in maintaining his post until the end. Andrew Latimer, a chief steward, gave his own life-jacket to a woman without one, then continued to load passengers into boats until they had all been launched. The five postal clerks hauled sacks of registered mail – many weighing up to 45 kilograms (100 pounds) – up one level after another to keep ahead of the rising water. All five lost their lives, and it is estimated that 3,364 sacks of mail went down with the ship. Similarly, Jack Phillips and Harold Bride remained at their wireless even after Captain Smith told them and other crew members to save themselves.

Meanwhile, *Titanic*'s stern had risen higher out of the water because of the sinking bow, and at about 2:17am, a massive roar was heard by those

in the lifeboats as the increasing angle caused all the ship's fittings and furniture suddenly to crash towards the bow. Moments later, the stern approached a 45° angle, maintaining that position for some 30 seconds before the lights finally failed. Then, the two front funnels toppled into the water, throwing out clouds of steam and soot. Finally, with a sound like thunder, the stress on the hull snapped *Titanic* in two between the third and fourth funnels. The bow slid beneath the

ABOVE: *Chief Officer Henry F Wilde had the misfortune of being transferred over to* Titanic *at the last moment from* Olympic, *joining in Southampton. Previous Chief Officer William Murdoch became First Officer instead.*

THE TRAGEDY OF THIRD-CLASS

Although the legend that third-class passengers were locked below decks is untrue, they still suffered far greater losses than the upper classes. Stewards were not as thorough or prompt in getting third-class passengers to the boat deck, and a lack of familiarity with the layout of the upper decks made escape upwards more difficult. Then, at points, men were prevented access to the boat deck, although women were allowed up. As a result, although roughly 62 per cent of first-class was saved, and almost 59 per cent of second-class, only some 25 per cent of third-class passengers lived to tell the tale.

❝It was about two o'clock in the morning when the *Titanic* finally sank, there were two terrific explosions and several loud screams as she went down bows first. As she sank the lights gradually faded as if someone was slowly turning off the current. There was a deathly silence in the boat, and even then no one realized the great loss of life. We pulled away in silence.❞

– *J. Witters*

ABOVE LEFT: *This diagram shows the different decks on Titanic, and gives an idea of the complicated routes third-class passengers would have had to follow to reach the boat deck.*

ABOVE RIGHT: *A diagram showing how, in her final tragic moments, Titanic's stern raised out of the water, her hull broke in two and she sank beneath the surface.*

surface and planed diagonally downwards, while the stern seemed to settle briefly before plunging to the bottom.

Some of those still aboard were sucked to the depths with the ship, while others were simply thrown into the freezing water. Both Collapsibles A and B were washed overboard, with those already loaded into the former swept out of it. Others managed to climb aboard or grab onto its sides in the midst of the chaos, and it remained afloat, although partly flooded.

Collapsible B also saved many lives, although it fell into the water upside down. Lightoller and Colonel Archibald Gracie were sucked under by the force of the sinking ship, both barely reaching the surface again, Lightoller only when thrust up by a blast of air forced from a ventilator. They managed to reach Collapsible B and pull themselves onto the bottom of the upturned boat with some 30 other men, who struggled all night to stay aboard.

Also there was Harold Bride, who was trapped in an air pocket under the boat for 45 minutes, then had to hang onto its side before being pulled out of the water by those in Lifeboat 12. Not so fortunate was his colleague Jack Phillips, who reached the boat, but died of exposure during the night. Tragically, the same was true of countless others.

“We knew that the ship had struck something but took no notice. Work was going on as if nothing had happened. When at twenty to two the ship seemed as if she had started again and flung us off our feet Mr. Sloan & Mr. Parr said to me 'Go up and see how things are going on and come and tell us.' Telling you the truth Sir, I had a job to get up the engine room ladder. I had to go up the dummy tunnel, there is a doorway there. The sight I saw I can hardly realise it. The second funnel was under water and all the boats had left the ship. I could not get back as the boat was sinking fast. We did not know they were all at boat stations. I am sure that that was where Mr. Parr was and so would I have been if they had not sent me up. ”

– Alfred White

ABOVE: *An artist's impression of* Titanic *in her death throes before going to the bottom of the sea. In reality, the night was pitch black, several of her funnels came off, and she split in two.*

TOP RIGHT: *An illustration from* The Illustrated London News *showing Captain Smith handing a baby to survivors on Collapsible B before returning towards the wreckage. There is no evidence this actually occurred.*

THE FATE OF CAPTAIN SMITH

Captain Smith does not appear to have followed any unified course of action in the final two hours aboard *Titanic*. He was last seen with certainty near the bridge after 2:00am, having told crew members to save themselves. Several legends sprang up about his final moments. One stated he carried a baby out to one of the boats before swimming back into the maelstrom. Another indicated he reached Collapsible B, but finding it overcrowded, simply swam away. Most likely, however, he remained on the bridge and went down with his ship.

ABOVE: *A reproduction of the* Titanic *as her bow sinks beneath the water line and the stern begins to raise out of the water. The image appears rather peaceful, but in reality the decks would have been full of frightened passengers and crew.*

NEXT PAGE: *Marschall's interpretation of the moment* Titanic *sunk.*

⟡ LANDING CARD ⟡

RIGHT: A landing card issued to *Titanic* survivor Edwina Trout so that she could disembark from *Carpathia* and clear immigration in New York. Although British by birth, she remained in the United States after the tragedy, first in Massachusetts and later in California.

CUNARD LINE.

SECOND CABIN.

LANDING OR CUSTOM CARD.

Name *Edwina Trout*

(and .... members of family).

List *3*   Number on List *13*

S.S. *Carpathia ex Titanic*

From Liverpool *Southampton ...... Apr 18 ...* 19 *12*

To be exhibited to IMMIGRATION OFFICIALS at NEW YORK and surrendered at Steamer's Dock on disembarking.

HYDROGRAPHIC OFFICE,
WASHINGTON, D. C.

DAILY MEMORANDUM

No. 1013.   April 15, 1912.

NORTH ATLANTIC OCEAN

OBSTRUCTIONS OFF THE AMERICAN COAST.

Mar. 28 - Lat 24° 20', lon 80° 02', passed a broken spar projecting about 3 feet out of water, apparently attached to sunken wreckage.--EVELYN (SS) Wright.

OBSTRUCTIONS ALONG THE OVER-SEA ROUTES.

Apr 7 - Lat 35° 20', lon 59° 40', saw a lowermast covered with marine growth.--ADRIATICO (It. ss), Cevascu.

ICE REPORTS.

Apr 7 - Lat 45° 10', lon 56° 40', ran into a strip of field ice about 3 or 4 miles wide extending north and south as far as could be seen. Some very heavy pans were seen.--ROSALIND (Br ss), Williams.

Apr 10 - Lat 41° 50', lon 50° 25', passed a large ice field a few hundred feet wide and 15 miles long extending in a NNE direction.--EXCELSIOR (Ger ss). (New York Herald)

COLLISION WITH ICEBERG - Apr 14 - Lat 41° 46', lon 50° 14', the British steamer TITANIC collided with an iceberg seriously damaging her bow; extent not definitely known.

Apr 14 - The German steamer AMERIKA reported by radio telegraph passing two large icebergs in lat 41° 27', lon 50° 08'.--TITANIC (Br ss).

Apr 14 - Lat 42° 06', lon 49° 43', encountered extensive field ice and saw seven icebergs of considerable size.--PISA (Ger ss).

J. J. K N A P P

Captain, U. S. Navy,
Hydrographer.

⟡ US NAVY MEMO ⟡

LEFT: One of the first reports of the collision was this daily memo from Captain JJ Knapp, the Hydrographer of the US Navy, calmly reporting the collision of *Titanic* with an iceberg and noting previous reports of bergs or heavy ice.

❧ W T STEAD ❧

ABOVE: At the time, journalist William Thomas Stead
was one of the most famous people to lose their life in
the *Titanic* disaster.

1, COCKSPUR STREET, S.W.
"Oceanic House."
TELEGRAPHIC ADDRESS "VESSELS, LONDON."
38, LEADENHALL STREET, E.C.
LONDON
TELEGRAPHIC ADDRESS "ISMAY, LONDON."
CANUTE ROAD, SOUTHAMPTON.
TELEGRAPHIC ADDRESS "ISMAY, SOUTHAMPTON"
9, BROADWAY, NEW YORK.
TELEGRAPHIC ADDRESS "ISMAY, NEW YORK."
84, STATE St. BOSTON.
TELEGRAPHIC ADDRESS "ISMAY, BOSTON."
118, NOTRE DAME St WEST, MONTREAL.
TELEGRAPHIC ADDRESS "ISMAY, MONTREAL."
21, PIAZZA DELLA BORSA, NAPLES.
TELEGRAPHIC ADDRESS "ISMAY, NAPLES."
VIA ALLA NUNZIATA, No 18, GENOA.
TELEGRAPHIC ADDRESS "ISMAY, GENOA."
PARIS AGENT: NICHOLAS MARTIN, 9, RUE SCRIBE.
TELEGRAPHIC ADDRESS "ISMAY, PARIS."
30, JAMES St, LIVERPOOL.
TELEGRAPHIC ADDRESS "ISMAY, LIVERPOOL."

Sir H.Ll. Smith H.Ll.S
The President.
Aps. 16.'12

This should be registered

Mr. Reg.

LIVERPOOL, April 15th 1912.

Sir Walter J. Howell, K.C.B.
      Marine Department,
            Board of Trade,
                  Whitehall,
                        London.S.W.

Dear Sir,

            We beg to thank you for your telegram reading

as follows and to express our appreciation of the kind enquiry

contained therein:-

            "Trust rumours about 'Titanic' unfounded pray send me news
      "most anxious . "

            We confirm our reply as under and will not fail

to keep you posted with any reliable information we may receive:-

            "Many thanks for your telegram for Mr. Ismay who is on
      "board 'Titanic' so far our only information is telegram
      "from New York as follows begins"Newspaper wireless reports
      "advise Titanic collision iceberg lat 41.46 north long
      "50.14 west women being put lifeboats steamer Virginian
      "expects reach Titanic ten a.m. today Olympic Baltic pro-
      "ceeding Titanic we have no direct information'ends. "

                        We are,

                              Yours faithfully,

                              For ISMAY IMRIE & CO.

P.S.   We have since telegraphed you as under:-

      "Underwriters have message from New York that 'Virginian'
      "is standing by 'Titanic' and that there is no danger of
      "loss of life. "

      "Latest word from Press agency 'Titanic' proceeding
      "to Cape Race all passengers transferred presumably to
      "'Virginian.' "

1, COCKSPUR STREET, S.W.
"Oceanic House"
TELEGRAPHIC ADDRESS:"VESSELS, LONDON:
38, LEADENHALL STREET, E.C.
LONDON.
TELEGRAPHIC ADDRESS "ISMAY, LONDON."
CANUTE ROAD, SOUTHAMPTON.
TELEGRAPHIC ADDRESS "ISMAY, SOUTHAMPTON".
9, BROADWAY, NEW YORK.
TELEGRAPHIC ADDRESS:"ISMAY, NEW YORK."
84, STATE ST, BOSTON.
TELEGRAPHIC ADDRESS "ISMAY, BOSTON."
118, NOTRE DAME ST WEST, MONTREAL.
TELEGRAPHIC ADDRESS "ISMAY, MONTREAL".
21, PIAZZA DELLA BORSA, NAPLES.
TELEGRAPHIC ADDRESS"ISMAY, NAPLES."
VIA ALLA NUNZIATA, N° 18, GENOA.
TELEGRAPHIC ADDRESS "ISMAY, GENOA".
PARIS AGENT: NICHOLAS MARTIN, 9, RUE SCRIBE.
TELEGRAPHIC ADDRESS "ISMAY, PARIS."
30, JAMES ST, LIVERPOOL.
TELEGRAPHIC ADDRESS, "ISMAY, LIVERPOOL"

G.
E. D.

LIVERPOOL, April 16th, 1912.

Sir Walter J. Howell, K.C.B.
    Marine Department, Board of Trade,
        7, Whitehall Gardens,
            London. S.W.

Dear Sir,

        Further to our communication of yesterday we were

extremely sorry to have to send you the following wire this

morning :-

        "Referring telegram yesterday 'Titanic' deeply grieved
        "say that during night we received word steamer foundered
        "about 675 souls mostly women and children saved".

which we now beg to confirm.

                    Yours faithfully,

                For ISMAY, IMRIE & CO:

 ISMAY LETTERS

ABOVE, LEFT: Two letters to Sir Walter Howell of the Marine
Department of the Board of Trade from Ismay, Imrie & Co.
The first indicates that it appears there is no danger of loss of
life. An about-face the next day confirms the tragedy.

BELOW, RIGHT: An account by Henrik Naess of his time aboard
Samson. He claims those aboard saw rockets launched by *Titanic*.

THE "SAMSON" and the "TITANIC"

From a manuscript account of his experiences prepared by Mr. Henrik Naess.

———————————

(Translation certified under Norwegian Government Authority)

———————————

After I had given up the "Munroe" I worked as a bosun on a coastal vessel for a short while. I then had some ear trouble which forced me to stay ashore without work for some time during the winter. At one time, I was quite deaf. After Christmas 1912 I received two good offers of work. One was a skipper of a small boat from Kristiansund plying the herring trade. The other was a job as mate on a large sealing vessel belonging to a Trondheim group. I chose the latter.

The sealing vessel was a large bark-rigged ship with a powerful engine and six - eight boats. Her name was "Samson" and she was bound for Newfoundland on a sealing expedition. At the moment she was lying in Tonsberg and when I arrived on board the men were already busy carrying equipment and stores on board.

From Tonsberg we proceeded to Oslo where "Samson" was docked and painted under the waterline, then we returned to Tonsberg where we took in coal and on 8th February we departed, passed Tonsberg Tonne and proceeded south along the shore. At Lindesnes we set course north of the Orkneys. The wind was northwesterly and we used the engine. We were altogether 45 men on board, and the Master, Captain Ring, was every inch a seaman. He was also an arctic expert.

When we had passed the Orkneys, the course was altered towards the west and we were in the Atlantic. We approached Newfoundland and could begin to expect ice. The temperature in the sea was measured every hour, and when it approached 0° centigrade, every half hour. We had to do this because the fog was so dense that we were unable to see anything. We proceeded under these conditions for a while, and then we entered so-called fishball ice - ice which the sea has broken to bits against the floes. And half an hour later we reached the actual icefloe. It was quite compact and impossible to penetrate. Anyway we did not intend to do so as we could not expect to find any seals there. We turned towards the southwest and proceeded on that course until noon the next day. By then, our dead reckoning and noon observations showed our position to be on a level with Cape Hatteras (?), and indeed we saw the Cape too. The whole afternoon we continued southwest until dusk. Then we entered the ice and stopped for the night. The weather was now quite clear and calm, the stars were shining, and there was a slight swell.

We had six-hour watches, with four gunners on each watch. Two of them were on watch on the bridge, so that we always had one man on each side of the bridge.

I was on duty that evening, but was sitting together with the Captain in his cabin, having a rum toddy and an evening pipe. A little before twelve I went up on deck waiting to be relieved. While walking about on deck I noticed two big stars hanging low in the sky to the south.

They seem pretty low, those stars, I said to the watchman on the bridge. Climb up to the crow's nest and see what it might be.

I thought it might be American sealers lying at the edge of the ice. The man climbed up and turned his telescope towards the stars.

/Over............

-2-

They are not stars, he called down to me. They are lights. And I see lots of lights.

A moment passed, then suddenly some rockets shot up. Then just as suddenly, all the lights went out and it was dark. We could no longer see anything.

Now, our *position was such that we were scared that we might be caught violating the territorial limit. The lights out there meant that the Americans were close, and when the lights were put out we immediately thought that they had perhaps observed us and would try to catch us. The rockets were probably signals to other vessels further away. We therefore turned about and started to manoeuver northwards in order to get out of sight. When dawn came we were quite a distance away and could not see any ships nor any sign that there had been ships nearby. We passed a lot of big icebergs, some of them enormous, up to 200 feet high. They passed us like great floating islands.

This interlude was soon forgotten and we continued north. Our catch was poor and we began to feel downhearted because we needed quite a number of seals if each man was to make a profit, considering how many we were. We spent eight days here, and then decided to proceed up the Denmark Strait to try the crested seal. We turned east, got a good wind and after four days sailing we encountered the ice inside the Davis Strait. But here too we cruised around without much luck.

Finally the ice began to settle round us. We discussed whether we should go out or remain fast in the ice - we decided on the latter course. We stayed there for a while, but as the ice refused to break up again we had to butt our way out.

We had the wind and sea straight against the edge of the ice, and the ship received many heavy blows. But that did not matter because "Samson" was one of the strongest and largest of Norway's arctic vessels. She was later bought by Admiral Byrd and used on his Antarctic expedition. The rim of the ice was moving violently owing to the action of the sea, and as we broke out we collided with an icefloe which was thrust at us by the sea. The steel strips round the bow snapped and six of the planks in the ice-doubling were knocked loose from the bow. Sea-council was held and we decided to put into a port in Iceland for refuge. There we passed up the Icefjord and beached the vessel to see if the damage could be repaired.

We contacted the shipowners and were instructed to return home and call at Kristiansund for further orders. We therefore immediately started to bolt the ice-doubling in position and while we were waiting for high tide in order to refloat the ship, the Captain and I were invited for supper at the home of the local consul.

Have you heard the last bad news?, asked the consul.

No, we had not.

Well, the big new passenger ship "Titanic", while on her maiden voyage, had collided with an iceberg and had sunk. Lots of lives - more than 1500 - had been lost.

When did this happen? I asked. Something was beginning to dawn on me.

---

*The original passage reads: "Nu la vi slik til at vi var redd vi kunde bli tatt for krenkelse av territorialgrensen". It consequently appears that the reference to the Samson's "position" was not intended to be taken in the strictly navigational sense, but rather as bearing upon her situation. In a letter dated 18th November, 1939, addressed to the Norwegian explorer, Adolf Hoel, Mr. Naess is understood to have explained that the Samson had been sealing in Labrador without licence or permission to do so.

During the night between the 14th and 15th April. The consul went out and found a newspaper. There we could read the whole report and all the information, including the position.

I took the newspaper with me and when we had returned on board I turned up the log at that date and compared our position with the position reported for the "Titanic". The date, hour and position corresponded exactly with our own entries.

Now we understood why we had seen the lights and the rockets. We had been 10 nautical miles away from the "Titanic" when she went down. There we had been lying with our big ship and eight fine sealing boats - in fair, calm weather. Imagine what we could have done to save lives - if only we had had the slightest idea of what was happening just in front of us. Had we only had a radio, for instance. ....

AFLOAT IN THE MIDDLE OF THE OCEAN

Where *Titanic* had been so shortly before, the ocean was now dotted only with 20 boats, bits of flotsam and hundreds of individuals in the icy water crying for help. Although far better off than those in the water – most of whom quickly died – the people in the boats still did not know when help would arrive, or if it were on the way at all. Those in the boats were a mixed bag from the broad selection of people aboard the ship, and accordingly behaved in widely different fashions.

No stranger tale unfolded than in Lifeboat 6, where Quartermaster Robert Hichens seemed more concerned with asserting authority than saving lives. When Major Arthur Peuchen let himself down the ropes to join the boat, Hichens quickly assigned him to row, along with lookout Frederick Fleet, while taking the tiller himself. The quartermaster had initially been ordered to take the boat to the mysterious ship in the distance, but before they could do so an officer called for them to come back alongside. Hichens ignored the order, and instead decided to get as far away from *Titanic* as possible before she sank.

Fleet and Peuchen, however, had difficulty propelling the boat alone, and Hichens refused to row, so Margaret Brown grabbed an oar and began rowing herself. She was quickly joined by several other women.

Throughout the night, even after the mystery ship disappeared and *Titanic* went down, Mrs Brown managed to keep up the spirits of the party, despite the quartermaster displaying an ever-increasing attitude of doom and gloom. When they met Lifeboat 16, in which a stoker was suffering terribly from the cold, "Molly" Brown stood to the fore, wrapping her fur coat around him and likely saved his life.

In Lifeboat 8, the 33-year-old Countess of Rothes had a similar impact, both rowing and taking charge of the tiller. So grateful was Able-bodied Seaman (AB) Thomas Jones for her spirit and labour that he later took the number plate from the boat and gave it to her.

Meanwhile, when Lifeboat 4 finally reached the water, one of the crew called out that they were in need of another man to row. Quartermaster Walter Perkis immediately slid down the ropes and took charge. Despite objections from some of the nervous passengers, he guided the boat towards *Titanic*'s stern, hoping to pick up more people at

GOING BACK FOR SURVIVORS

Although the frantic cries of those in the water disturbed many in the lifeboats, most remained safely at a distance to avoid being swamped by the desperate people. In Lifeboat 8, the Countess of Rothes and three others proposed going back to help, but were overruled. Similarly, in Lifeboat 1, fireman Charles Hendrickson was unable to convince the others. In the initial period after the sinking, only Lifeboat 4, under Walter Perkis, made a serious effort to collect others; seven or eight were rescued, although two of them died that night.

LEFT: *With Quartermaster Robert Hichens standing in the stern, Lifeboat 6 approaches the rescuing* Carpathia. *Hichens' reputation was severely damaged by his behaviour after* Titanic *sank, and in 1914 he moved to South Africa to work as a harbour-master.*

HANGING ON TO COLLAPSIBLE B

Of the survivors, few had a harder night than those on Collapsible B. So many men hauled themselves aboard the overturned boat that it was in constant danger of sinking. To the horror of Archibald Gracie, some then prevented others from climbing on; baker Charles Joughin, for example, was pushed away until someone aboard died, opening a space for him. Eventually, Lightoller organized the men so that they could lean from one side of the boat to the other on his command, keeping the collapsible evenly balanced and helping to avoid foundering.

the rear companionway. Finding the doors under water, he nevertheless saved two crewmen before moving away from the ship.

One individual who had to wait a good deal longer for help was saloon steward Harold Phillimore. Having jumped from the boat deck in *Titanic*'s final seconds, he clung atop a piece of wreckage with another man until the other slipped into the frigid waters. After about an hour and a half, those aboard Lifeboat 14 under Fifth Officer Harold Lowe – seeking any survivors among the floating bodies – heard Phillimore's calls for help and pulled him into their boat.

One of the most disturbing stories emanated from Lifeboat 1, which had only 12 of its 40 spaces occupied. First, there was friction between lookout George Symons, who was nominally in charge, and first-class passenger Henry Stengel, who wanted to be. Then, as the occupants of the lifeboat watched the ship go down several hundred yards away, the idea was broached about going back to help those in the water. Lucile, Lady Duff Gordon, objected, and Symons refused to order it, so they remained where they were. It later emerged that Sir Cosmo Duff Gordon had offered each of the seven crewmen £5. He insisted this was to help replace their lost kit, but others alleged it was so they would not take the boat to where it could be swamped. True or not, the charge haunted Sir Cosmo for the rest of his life. Meanwhile, another man who would be criticized for his actions that night – J Bruce Ismay – sat silently on Collapsible C, facing away from the ship he had done so much to create.

❝ I was swimming along in the night, when suddenly I saw far away a sort of raft, half submerged, loaded with people. It took me I guess about half an hour to reach it. At first they would not let me get on, but I succeeded never the less. We were about twenty people there, men and women, with water up to our thighs. We had balance ourselves, from left to right, to prevent the raft from turning over. I remained there six hours, in my shirt, freezing to death. I almost let myself go and fall into the water two or three times, but the thought of you prevented me from doing it. ❞

– George Rheims

ABOVE: *Amongst those who later visited the site of the tragedy were seamen who attempted to salvage Collapsible B. Most of the lifeboats were taken to New York.*

“ The morale of the people in the boat was excellent at all times, and was greatly assisted by the endeavours of a Mrs Brown, who sang and joked with everyone, she carried with her a little Toy Pig which played a little melody when its tail was turned, this amused the passengers immensely.

We pulled around hopefully when, with a great feeling of elation we sighted a ship at about six o'clock, at first we all thought that it was the *Olympic*, but when she finally closed on us we distinguished her as the *Carpathia*. With thanks to God we boarded her. We were saved. ”

– J. Witters

“ The dear officer gave orders to row away from the sinking boat at least 200 yards, he afterwards, poor dear brave fellow, shot himself. We saw the whole thing, and watched that tremendous thing quickly sink, there was then terrible, terrible explosions, and all darkness, then followed the awful cries and screams of the 1600 dear souls, fighting for their lives in the water. Oh never shall I forget, that awful night, floating about the ocean in this little boat, freezing cold, & listening to this terrible suffering, we all prayed all night long, that help may come to us all, & how I thought of all my darlings, & those dear to me. ”

– Laura Mable Francatelli

“ I knew then we were soon going the distress signals then were going every second, so I thought if anyone asked me again to go I should do so, there was a big crush from behind me, at last they realized their danger, so I was pushed into the boat. I believe it was one of the last boats to leave. We had scarcely got clear when she began sinking rapidly. The rest is too awful to write about. We were in the boats all night. I took a turn to row. The women said I encouraged them, I was pleased. We picked up 30 men. Standing on an upturned boat, among them was one of our Officers, Mr. Lightoller, we then took charge until the *Carpathia* picked us up about 7 in the morning. I only hope I shall never have a like experience again. ”

– Mary Sloan

ABOVE: *Molly Brown, in a portrait taken 15 years after* Titanic *sank. Her actions on the night made her a celebrity and in 1914 she was even proposed as a potential Congressional candidate.*

TOP CENTRE: *Lucile, Lady Duff Gordon, set up a dress-making business after she was divorced from her first husband. Its remarkable success made her one of the leaders in the European fashion industry.*

TOP RIGHT: *The 33-year-old Countess of Rothes not only took the tiller of Lifeboat 8 and helped row, but was one of the most outspoken in favour of going back to save others.*

❧ RESCUED ❧

Within moments of receiving the emergency message from *Titanic*, Captain Arthur Rostron ordered his ship, the Cunard liner *Carpathia*, to speed towards the coordinates Jack Phillips had transmitted. Ordering all off-duty firemen and trimmers to the boilers, he drove the ship at a speed she had never before attained, nor ever would again: 17 knots – three more than what was considered her top rate. Adding extra lookouts, he maintained the pace even when *Carpathia* reached the region dotted with icebergs. At 3:00am, Rostron ordered rockets to be fired at 15-minute intervals, so survivors would know help was on the way. But at about 3:30am, reaching *Titanic*'s supposed position, he could see nothing, so, grimly, he proceeded on.

ABOVE: *Cottam and Bride worked all night so that* Titanic *survivors could contact loved ones. This telegram is from Edith Rosenbaum and reads "Safe* Carpathia, *notify mother".*

Lowe hoped to save as many people from the freezing water as possible, but knowing that his boat would be swamped if he went into the midst of the flailing mass, he waited until the cries had subsided. He then searched through the bobbing bodies and eventually picked up four survivors.

To those aboard the small boats in the middle of the icy ocean, the night seemed interminable, and the freezing temperatures threatened anybody still alive. When Collapsible A finally met Lowe's group of boats, the people in it were sitting in several feet of cold water, and as Lowe transferred them to the other boats, he found that three were dead. The minutes continued to tick by, but finally a light could be seen in the distance. *Carpathia* was approaching.

Just after 4:00am, Rostron ordered the engines stopped, and as his men searched the dark waters, a green light was seen 275 metres (300 yards) ahead. It was Lifeboat 2, which

was under the charge of Fourth Officer Joseph Boxhall; at 4:10am, Elizabeth Allen became the first survivor to be taken aboard. Shortly thereafter, Boxhall reported to Rostron that *Titanic* was gone.

As dawn came, the lifeboats began making their way towards *Carpathia*. Second Office Lightoller, still in charge of the balancing act on upturned Collapsible B, gained the attention of Lifeboat 12, which separated from Lowe's flotilla to pick them up. They then turned to the ship but, being so heavily loaded, made only slow progress. Meanwhile, many people, often too cold and numb to hold on to anything, were lifted by *Carpathia*'s crewmen and brought aboard in slings. It was a painfully slow process, and it was not until 8:10am that Lightoller, having guided Lifeboat 12 to the ship with 75 people in it, became the final person to reach safety.

At 8:30am, *Californian*, which had transmitted the ice warning that Phillips had

ignored, became the second ship to arrive. Leaving that vessel, under Captain Stanley Lord, to conduct a thorough search of the area, Rostron steamed west, towards New York. Despite suffering so severely from his lengthy time in the water that he had to be carried off *Carpathia* in New York, *Titanic* wireless officer Harold Bride in the meantime was co-opted to help Harold Cottam in the wireless room. The two worked non-stop sending messages from the survivors, transmitting an official list of the survivors and contacting White Star Line.

Meanwhile, one of *Carpathia*'s scheduled passengers, the artist Colin Campbell Cooper, produced two evocative paintings of the rescue. He and his wife also gave their cabin to three women from *Titanic*. It was a gesture repeated time and again, as those already aboard – who had been sailing for the Mediterranean – did their best to comfort the bereaved, before (for many of the latter) the dreadful ordeal continued ashore.

ABOVE: Carpathia *was never intended to rival the great luxury liners. Coming into service in 1903, she had vast refrigerated areas to transport various foods, but carried only second- and third-class passengers.*

SAVED:
THE STATISTICS

Just as there is no agreement as to how many people sailed on *Titanic*, the estimates of survivors vary significantly. After a head-count, Captain Rostron indicated that 705 boarded *Carpathia*. The British Board of Inquiry, however, arrived at the figure 711, whilst White Star's official list, published a week after the tragedy, claimed 757 people lived through it. More recent studies have arrived at other figures, but it is widely accepted that the number saved was roughly 700 out of approximately 2,200 aboard – meaning that more than two-thirds of those on *Titanic* died.

❝ The Wireless Man was on the raft the Officer asked what ships he had contact he said *Caledonia* and *Carpathia* would be on the spot at 4AM which was when she [was] sighted we began to shout but the Officer said she is four miles away save your breath. On board *Carpathia* Duff Gordon sent for his boat's crew and I saw Five Pound Note he gave to each one I took the liberty to tell one he would be sorry he had it. **❞**

– Walter Hurst

❝ The old S.S. *Carpathia* picked us up about 7 A.M on the 15th April. She took us to New York (took about 4 days I think). Quite a few survivors died on the *Carpathia*. The first night aboard there quite a few died from exposure and frost-bite. An officer asked me to go to the mortuary, four has died – he had an idea one of them was a member of the *Titanic* crew and 'perhaps I could identify him'. I jibbed, it may have been one of my mates. I had had enough. **❞**

– George Kemish

TOP LEFT: *All that was left of* Titanic *when* Carpathia *reached New York was her lifeboats, which were left at the White Star pier before Rostron docked his ship at the Cunard pier.*

ABOVE: *A boatload of survivors – their anxious wait now over – prepare to board* Carpathia, *as one seaman from the rescuing ship looks on from above.*

I saw a Swedish couple and their five children kiss each other goodbye, and then they all jumped overboard. (This was while I was still on the *Titanic*.) After we were in lifeboats, those who had papers or any article that could burn, lit these, thus making flares. In this way the lifeboats kept going in the same direction, and not getting scattered in various directions. In the morning we were sighted by the *Carpathia*, and were taken aboard her in the early hours, about 8.30 a.m. I might also add that, though the ocean was quite calm, two lifeboats did overturn – at least that is all I saw capsize. **99**

– Anna Kincaid

66 There were several ladies in the boats. They were slightly injured about the arms and things of that king, of course; although I must say, from the very start, all these people behaved magnificently. As each boat came alongside everyone was calm, and they kept perfectly still in their boats. They were quiet and orderly, and each person came up the ladder, or was pulled up, in turn as they were told off. There was no confusion whatever among the passengers. They behaved magnificently – ever one of them. As they came aboard, they were, of course, attended too… **99**

– Captain Rostron

CAPTAIN ROSTRON'S PREPARATIONS

Captain Rostron knew that every moment *Titanic*'s passengers were left outside might prove fatal. Therefore, as *Carpathia* steamed forwards, he made detailed rescue preparations. Rostron had the ship's three doctors establish separate medical stations in the dining rooms. Public areas and cabins were stocked with blankets, warm clothing, food and hot drinks. Electric lights were strung over the sides to make boarding easier, and ladders, chair slings, nets and even bags for small children were readied to help or hoist the survivors up. Even the cranes were prepared so they could haul up any luggage or mail that might have been saved.

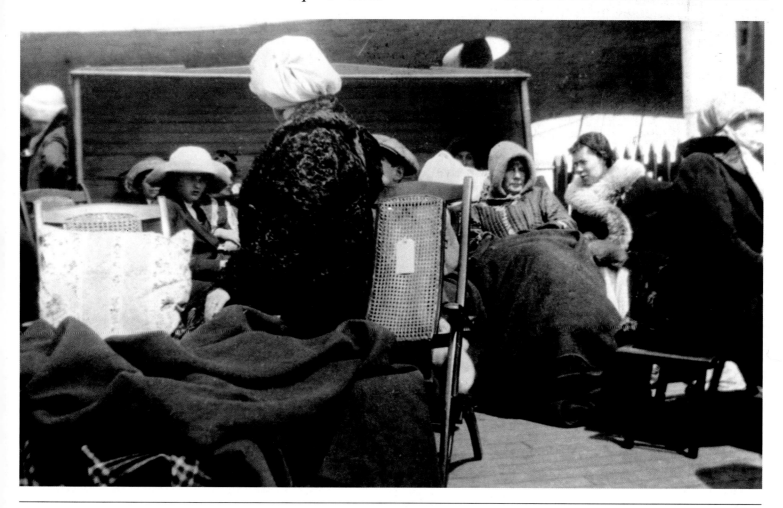

ABOVE: *Those rescued from the clutches of the ocean huddle with blankets and heavy clothes aboard* Carpathia. *The passengers from the rescuing ship made every effort to comfort and aid the survivors.*

TOP RIGHT: *A special medal issued to Captain Rostron. It reads: "For heroically saving the seven hundred and four passengers of the* Titanic *in mid-ocean. The thanks of Congress. July 6, 1912. To Arthur Henry Rostron."*

THE SURVIVORS

According to Captain Rostron, there were now 705 extra people aboard *Carpathia*: 705 individuals thankful to be alive, but 705 confused souls, mourning for lost family, friends and colleagues. Many were also physically injured, mentally exhausted and distressed about lost possessions. Their emotions were in a whirl, while for four hours Rostron made his way through the treacherous ice fields about which *Titanic* had been warned.

There were, of course, those who had, beyond hope, found loved ones they had thought lost. Ruth Dodge and her four-year-old son had been in Lifeboat 5, the second one sent out. It was not until her son said that he had seen his daddy aboard *Carpathia* but had been playing a game by hiding from him, that she discovered her husband had reached safety in Lifeboat 13.

Equally fortunate was Nellie Becker, who was travelling with her three children. When Lifeboat 11 was loaded, four-year-old Marion and one-year-old Richard were placed in it, and it was declared full. Nellie screamed that she needed to be with her children, and she was allowed in, but her daughter Ruth, aged 12, was not. Ruth eventually went into Lifeboat 13, and, like the Dodges, was unexpectedly but luckily reunited with her family aboard *Carpathia*.

Leah Aks, a third-class passenger born in Poland and travelling to join her husband, had one of the more traumatic ordeals of those in the lifeboats. As she waited for Lifeboat 11, one of the stewards suddenly grabbed her 10-month-old baby, Frank, and literally tossed him into the boat. When Leah tried to retrieve him, she was restrained by other stewards, who thought she was attempting to push her way onto the boat. Soon thereafter, the now-distraught woman was seated in Lifeboat 13, where Selena Rogers Cook and Ruth Becker tried to comfort her. Hours later, aboard *Carpathia*, Leah and Selena passed a woman holding a baby, whom Leah recognized as Frank, but the woman – supposedly either Elizabeth Nye or Argene del Carlo – claimed the baby as her own. Leah and Selena went to Captain Rostron, and after Leah described a birthmark on Frank's chest, he was returned to her.

Two children not so easily reunited with their parents were Michel and Edmond Navratil, aged three and two. As increasingly desperate people

ABOVE: *A badge for a steward from First Class. On its reverse side is engraved the name "Tommy", which is presumably the name of the steward who wore it.*

THE TALE OF J BRUCE ISMAY

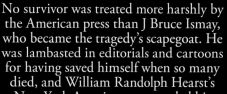

No survivor was treated more harshly by the American press than J Bruce Ismay, who became the tragedy's scapegoat. He was lambasted in editorials and cartoons for having saved himself when so many died, and William Randolph Hearst's New York American surrounded his photo with pictures of widows of those lost, referring to him as 'J Brute Ismay". The British were kinder, the inquiry finding him free of any fault, and many praising him for helping load women into boats before his own departure. Nonetheless, he remained guilt-ridden for the rest of his life.

❝ How lucky we were to be alive and even fed. But many were very fussy & annoying & stealing was really bad. Seemed everyone lost things both the regular passengers & any who brought anything with them. Mother made dresses for Margery Collyer & me out of a blue blanket and #50 thread sewing them by hand. Kept us warm but we sure looked funny, now as I look back…The things I saw are as plain in my mind as if they were printed on my brain. Guess I was very lucky having the kind of mother I had, for she was a tower of strength to lots who were sort of falling apart and a most practical psychologist in her own way. ❞

– Bertha Watt

TOP: *Portrait of J Bruce Ismay.*

ABOVE: *Male survivors of the Titanic disaster all show the same hopeless look. Many of the men who survived were never viewed or treated the same again.*

had crushed around Collapsible D in the moments before it was launched, second-class passenger Michel Hoffman had passed the two children through the stewards to the boat. But Hoffman went down with *Titanic*, and after *Carpathia* arrived in New York, the story of the two orphans was carried in newspapers around the world. Only then did it transpire that Hoffman, whose real name was Navratil, had stolen his sons from their mother – from whom he was unhappily separated – hoping she would join them all in the United States. In May, White Star Line arranged Marcelle Navratil's passage to New York, and she was able to take her two boys back to France.

Another son who lost his father was 21-year-old R Norris Williams. When *Titanic* began to go down, he and his father tried to swim away from the ship. To his amazement, Williams came face to face with Gamon de Pycombe, the award-winning bulldog of first-class passenger Robert W Daniels, which was doing likewise. Williams' father died when a funnel collapsed on him, but the subsequent wave helped push the son towards Collapsible A, onto which he was pulled. On *Carpathia*, one of the doctors recommended amputating Williams' legs, which had been severely damaged by the cold water. Williams ignored the advice, and eventually was able to resume his tennis career.

Meanwhile, the hundreds of survivors travelling aboard *Carpathia* endured thunderstorms, heavy rain and thick fog on the painfully slow, woeful voyage to New York. There, on 18 April, before some 30,000 onlookers, Rostron eased his ship up to the Cunard pier. From here, it was the first step for the former *Titanic* passengers in making a very different entrance to the New World to the one they expected.

COFFINS AND CORPSES

Within hours of *Titanic* sinking, White Star initiated an attempt to recover the bodies of those who died. On 17 April, the cable ship *Mackay-Bennett* left Halifax, Nova Scotia, with more than 100 coffins and several (tonnes) tons of ice for preserving. In a week-long search, 306 bodies were found: 116 so totally unrecognizable that they were buried at sea and 190 that were brought back to Halifax. In the following weeks three other ships found another 22 bodies. In total, 150 victims were buried in cemeteries in Halifax and 59 were claimed by relatives and buried elsewhere.

ABOVE: *The men of* Mackay-Bennett *had the most disheartening – and gruesome – job of all: finding bodies that told the terrible facts of the tragedy.*

"…soon after that, about five o'clock we saw the mast lights of the *Carpathia* on the horizon – & then the headlights – & then the portholes & then we knew we should be saved. We had to go up on a rope ladder on the side of the *Carpathia* (I don't know how I did it), and then we were taken on board & given coffee & brandy – but as our boat was about the sixteenth or eighteenth to arrive all the berths were given away before I reached there & so I had to stay in the Library for the four days & nights before we reached New York – & there were no brushes or combs to be had – nor toothbrushes as these were all sold in a minute."

– *Mary Hewlett*

"At eight o'clock in the morning, a life-boat from the *Titanic* came to rescue us and took us on board the *Carpathia* where we were wonderfully taken care of. I found everyone on the dock. I find it difficult to walk, my feet being slightly bruised. Here I am settled at Harry's place and I think that a few day's rest will do me a lot of good. I admit that I am a little tired and you must excuse me if I end this letter here, a little abruptly."

– *George Rheims*

TOP: *Third Officer Herbert Pittman (in the pale cap) speaks to Second Officer Charles Lightoller (with the pipe) just after their return to Liverpool aboard* Adriatic *on 11 May.*

ABOVE: *When most of the surviving crew of* Titanic *arrived in Plymouth on 29 April, they were temporarily kept from rejoining their families or friends while they were interviewed one by one by Board of Trade officials.*

HEROES OF THE TITANIC

More than 1,500 passengers and crew members of *Titanic* lost their lives on a cold April night in 1912. Read on to uncover tales of ten men and women who miraculously beat monumental odds or tragically sacrificed it all on the waves of the Atlantic ocean.

Despite the common misconception, RMS *Titanic* was never called 'unsinkable' in the run up to its infamous maiden voyage. In fact, it wasn't until after the sinking that it became known as such. It was 'practically unsinkable', but so was every other luxury liner of the same period. These ships just didn't sink – that was the end of it – and there was nothing special about *Titanic* in this regard. It was because of this general attitude of superiority over the sea that *Titanic* carried only enough lifeboats for half of the passengers on board, and none of the crew members were trained in how to conduct an proper evacuation. The officers, later criticised for releasing lifeboats half full, simply had no idea how many people could safely board the boats. Nobody had the slightest notion that the ship would, or even could, sink.

With no procedures in place to protect them and a ship completely unprepared for evacuation, when *Titanic* hit an iceberg on 12 April 1912, those on board had to fend for themselves. For some, death was inevitable, but for others it was a noble choice – such as the devoted wife who refused to leave her husband, and the band that played until the final moment. In less than three hours, hundreds of lives were changed, and more were ended. From penniless immigrants to multi-millionaires, every person on board had a life, a story and a destiny. Their tales of heroism, sacrifice and survival have intrigued people for more than 100 years; these are just ten of them.

Joseph's daughter, Louise, became one of the oldest survivors of the Titanic *disaster, dying in 1998 aged 87.*

JOSEPH LAROCHE
SECOND-CLASS PASSENGER, 1886-1912
TITANIC'S FORGOTTEN BLACK HERO

Although Laroche was an educated man with an engineering degree, he struggled to find work because of rampant racism in France. So to pay for his daughter's medical bills, Laroche made the decision to return to his native Haiti with his family of two daughters, and another child on the way. The family first planned to travel on SS *France*, but changed their tickets to *Titanic* when they discovered they would not be able to dine with their children.

When *Titanic* struck the iceberg, Laroche quickly became aware that something was wrong. He woke his wife, Juliette, then put as many of their valuables as he could carry in his pockets. With their young daughters still sleeping, Laroche and Juliette carried the girls up to the deck. Joseph led his pregnant wife and daughters to a lifeboat, possibly lifeboat 8, safely, however, he could not follow them. Sadly, no more of Joseph's story is known. He died in the sinking and his body was never recovered. However, his wife and children survived, and Juliette went on to have a baby boy that she named Joseph in her late husband's honour.

❝ From penniless immigrants to multi-millionaires, every man, woman and child on board had a life, a story and a destiny ❞

" For some, death was inevitable, but for others it was a noble choice – such as the devoted wife who refused to leave her husband **"**

IDA & ISIDOR STRAUS

FIRST-CLASS PASSENGERS, 1845-1912/1849-1912

THE COUPLE THAT REFUSED TO BE SEPARATED

Ida and Isidor had always been a close couple. Isidor was often called abroad to travel as part of his role as a US representative for New York, or in his position as co-owner of department store Macy's, and he was constantly exchanging letters with his devoted wife. The couple had spent the winter together in Europe and found their way on to *Titanic* due to a coal strike in England.

When *Titanic* hit the iceberg, Ida and Isidor were both offered a place on a lifeboat, however, Isidor declined as there were still women and children on board. Despite his urges for his wife to climb in, she refused to leave without him, stating: "We have lived together for many years. Where you go, I go." Upon witnessing this display of affection, a survivor, Colonel Archibald Gracie IV, offered to help them onto a lifeboat together, but Isidor firmly said: "I will not go before the other men." Aged 67, Isidor believed that the younger men should be saved before himself. Ida made sure her maid was safely on a lifeboat, and handed over her fur coat saying that she would not be needing it. As the lifeboat lowered, those inside witnessed the couple standing arm and arm on the deck in "a most remarkable exhibition of love and devotion." Both died when the ship sank, and the couple's memorial service in New York was attended by 40,000 people.

A song telling the story of the dedicated wife called The Titanic's Disaster *became popular after the sinking.*

Rostron was later appointed Knight Commander of the Order of the British Empire.

SIR ARTHUR ROSTRON

CAPTAIN OF RMS CARPATHIA, 1869-1940

THE CAPTAIN WHO TRAVERSED THE ICE FOR SIGNS OF LIFE

Rostron is often forgotten as a hero of the *Titanic* disaster because he wasn't on board the ship that night, but thanks to his efforts, some 700 lives were saved from a terrible end in the ocean. After beginning his seafaring career aged 13, Rostron was placed in command of the steamship RMS *Carpathia*. The ship was travelling along its usual route between New York and Fiume when messages came in from the crew of the sinking *Titanic*. Rostron took immediate action, ordering the ship to divert its course to *Titanic*'s location.

This was no small act. Multiple other ships had received the distress signal, but due to the dense ice, had chosen to stop for the night. Rostron and his crew navigated through the ice at the maximum speed possible, avoiding 200-foot-tall icebergs. Miraculously, the ship made it through the treacherous water, and Rostron, an extremely pious man, later commented: "I can only conclude another hand than mine was on the helm."

It took about three and a half hours to reach the radioed position, but Rostron used this time to prepare the ship for survivors. He ensured there were enough blankets, food and drink ready, as well as medical assistance. Thanks to his expert leadership and bravery, *Carpathia* picked up 710 survivors. Rostron received much praise and was awarded a silver cup and gold medal from the survivors, as well as the congressional gold medal and an array of other awards.

❝ It took about three and a half hours to reach the radioed position, but Rostron used this time to prepare the ship for survivors ❞

CHARLES LIGHTOLLER
SECOND MATE, 1874-1952

THE OFFICER WHO BATTLED TO MAINTAIN ORDER IN CHAOS

Lightoller was no stranger to tragedies at sea. By 1895, aged 21, he had already experienced a shipwreck, fire at sea and a cyclone. After losing everything after a failed gold-prospecting venture, he became a hobo, riding the rails across Canada. By 1900, he had worked his way back home to England and joined the White Star Line, serving as Second Officer on *Titanic*'s maiden voyage.

Lightoller was off duty and in his pyjamas when he was woken by a vibration. Although he went out to the deck, he couldn't find anything wrong so returned to his cabin to await orders. He lay in his bunk until the fourth officer informed him of the water seeping into the ship. With the fate of the ship quickly becoming clear, he immediately set about organising evacuation on the lifeboats.

Because of the noise and panic, Lightoller was forced to use hand signals to convey messages while attempting to organise boats on the port side. Although some of the other officers were hesitant about lowering the boats so soon, Lightoller was a veteran of shipwrecks and eager to get them off as soon as possible. He persuaded as many women and children as possible onto the lifeboats and was very strict about allowing no men on board. He even went as far as to jump on to a

Lightoller was the most senior officer to survive the sinking.

lifeboat filled with men, threatening them with an unloaded pistol, shouting: "Get out of there, you damned cowards! I'd like to see every one of you overboard!" Although this action was later seen as controversial, many attribute Lightoller's strict command as preventing even more loss of life.

Lightoller remained on board even after being instructed to get on a lifeboat, replying "not damn likely." The officer was attempting to launch collapsible boat B when the boat deck flooded with water. The lifeboat floated off the deck upside down and Lightoller realised there was no more he could do, so he took a deep breath and dived into the water. He attempted to swim away but was sucked under and thrown against the grating of a ventilator shaft. Miraculously, a sudden blast from the boilers sent him to the surface and alongside collapsible boat B. He climbed on the boat and took charge of the 30-odd men clinging to it, calming the survivors and encouraging them to yell "boat ahoy." Throughout the night, he instructed the men to move their weight to keep the boat afloat. Thanks to his instruction, they were able to maintain this for hours. They were eventually rescued by a returning lifeboat, largely thanks to Lightoller blowing his whistle.

MARGARET BROWN
FIRST-CLASS PASSENGER, 1867-1932

THE UNSINKABLE FIREBRAND THAT FOUGHT FOR SURVIVORS

Also known as the 'Unsinkable Molly Brown', Margaret Brown was born the poor daughter of Irish immigrants. Although she dreamed of marrying a rich man, she fell in love with James Joseph Brown, a miner, and married him, later saying: "I decided that I'd be better off with a poor man whom I loved than with a wealthy one whose money had attracted me." The couple had two children and struggled with money. However, James eventually became superintendent of the mine and, thanks to his own enterprising ideas, became a hugely successful and wealthy businessman.

Margaret had boarded *Titanic* to visit her grandchild who was ill in New York. It was a last-minute decision, and many of her family members were unaware she was actually on board. When the ship hit the iceberg, the energetic woman leapt into action, helping several women and children into the lifeboats. After much persuasion, she eventually climbed aboard lifeboat 6 and encouraged the other women to row it with her, working hard to keep their spirits up. Quartermaster Robert Hichens was in charge of the lifeboat and Margaret reportedly clashed over the issue of going back for survivors. Margaret was determined to return for the people in the water as they still had room in the lifeboat, but Hichens

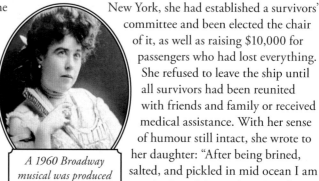

A 1960 Broadway musical was produced based on Brown's life.

feared that the people would swarm the boat and drag them down. It is unknown whether Margaret did manage to persuade him to go back or not.

However, it was her actions after the tragedy that drew the most attention. Upon boarding *Carpathia*, she assisted survivors, handing out food and blankets. By the time the ship arrived in New York, she had established a survivors' committee and been elected the chair of it, as well as raising $10,000 for passengers who had lost everything. She refused to leave the ship until all survivors had been reunited with friends and family or received medical assistance. With her sense of humour still intact, she wrote to her daughter: "After being brined, salted, and pickled in mid ocean I am now high and dry... I have had flowers, letters, telegrams from people until I am befuddled. They are petitioning Congress to give me a medal... If I must call a specialist to examine my head it is due to the title of Heroine of the *Titanic*."

Margaret went on to become a fierce activist of women's rights and was one of the first women to run for Congress before women even had the right to vote. During World War I she established a relief station for soldiers and was bestowed with medals and honours. After her death, she became known as the 'Unsinkable Molly Brown'.

THOMAS BYLES
SECOND-CLASS PASSENGER, 1870-1912

THE PRIEST PROVIDING COMFORT AMID THE PANIC

There are now efforts to ordain Father Byles as a saint.

Father Thomas Byles was a Catholic priest travelling on board *Titanic* to officiate the wedding of his younger brother. On the day of the sinking, he preached a sermon to second and third-class passengers about their new life in the USA and a need for a spiritual lifeboat to avoid temptation. Byles was frequently seen walking on deck praying, and it was there that he was stood when the ship hit the iceberg. When the ship began to sink, he helped third-class passengers reach the deck and escape on lifeboats. As the situation gradually worsened, he moved through the panicked crowds alone, giving absolution and reciting the rosary to the trapped passengers. Twice he was invited on board a lifeboat, and both times he refused to leave *Titanic*. As the passengers' deaths became imminent, Byles remained by their side, comforting them with words of god and granting absolution to those who sought it. When the ship went down, Byles was upon it, preaching the word of the Lord until the very end and bringing light to the darkest of times.

HAROLD BRIDE & JACK PHILLIPS
WIRELESS OFFICERS, 1890-1956/1887-1912

TWO MEN WHO REFUSED TO LEAVE THEIR POSTS UNTIL THE END

Harold Bride and Jack Phillips were both working as wireless officers on *Titanic* when it hit the iceberg. Bride had just woken up and was on his way to relieve an exhausted Phillips from a long night shift when the collision occurred. Unusually, neither man felt the tremor from the wireless room and it wasn't until the captain entered and told them to send out a distress signal that they were aware of any danger.

The two men, unaware of the gravity of the situation, joked as they sent out the distress call, with Bride kidding that Phillips should send out the new call 'SOS' rather than 'CQD', as it may be his last chance to send it. As the situation grew steadily more grim, Phillips worked tirelessly sending distress calls out on the wireless, while Bride dashed back and forth delivering messages between the wireless room and captain. Eventually, as the power began to cut out, the captain told them that they had done their duty and were relieved. As commotion and panic erupted on deck, Phillips continued working with dogged determination, and Bride later said: "I learned to love him that night, and I suddenly felt for him a great reverence to see him standing there sticking to his work while everybody else was raging about. I will never live to forget the work Phillips did for the last awful 15 minutes."

As Phillips continued to work, Bride fetched life jackets for both men. However, when their backs were turned, a crew member attempted to steal Phillips' jacket. Bride quickly grabbed the man, and Phillips knocked him out. As the room began to fill with water, they left the thief to his fate and raced out, finally abandoning their posts. At this point, the two officers split up. Bride headed towards the collapsible boat still on board and Phillips disappeared towards the aft. It was the last Bride would ever see of him. As Bride attempted to help free the collapsible boat, he was washed off the ship along with it. He managed to swim furiously away from the sinking vessel to avoid being sucked down, and climbed on the collapsible boat. Bride was eventually rescued aboard *Carpathia*, and although seriously injured, helped the ship's wireless officer, sending out personal messages from survivors until they docked.

Jack Phillips was just 25 when he died in the disaster.

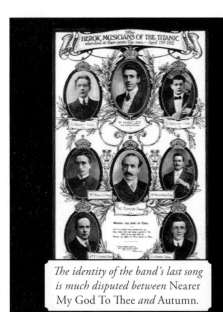

The identity of the band's last song is much disputed between Nearer My God To Thee *and* Autumn.

WALLACE HARTLEY & THE TITANIC BAND
MUSICIANS

THE FINAL PERFORMANCE OF EIGHT BRAVE MEN

The legend of the musicians on *Titanic* is one of the most well-known stories of heroism, and for good reason. The *Titanic* band featured eight men ranging from the age of 20 to 33, who all travelled in second class. Bandleader Wallace Hartley led them during their performances at tea time, Sunday services and an array of different occasions on board the ship, while a separate trio played outside the A La Carte restaurant and the Café Parisien. Therefore, when Hartley united the band on the night of the sinking, it was likely the first time they had all played together.

Shortly after midnight, when the lifeboats were beginning to be loaded, Hartley assembled the band in the first-class lounge and began to play. His aim was to calm the passengers. When the majority of people moved onto the boat deck, and the severity of the situation became clear, Hartley moved his band to the deck. As the ship filled with water and the decks began to slant, the band continued to play until their final moments. None of the band members survived, but the remarkable heroism and sacrifice shown by each of the men entered into legend.

THOMAS ANDREWS
TITANIC ARCHITECT, 1873-1912

THE BUILDER WHO WENT DOWN WITH HIS SHIP

Andrews was responsible for overseeing the plans of the *Olympic* and the *Titanic*. It was Andrews who recommended that the ship carry 46 lifeboats, rather than the 20 ultimately decided, as well as suggesting it have a double hill and watertight bulkheads up to B deck. Unfortunately, all these suggestions were ignored.

When the ship hit the iceberg, Andrews was immediately consulted. As the chief designer, he was familiar with every little detail of the vessel and so was perhaps the first person to understand the gravity of the situation. He informed Captain Smith that the ship sinking was a "mathematical certainty," and it would likely happen within an hour. He was also quick to warn the captain about the shortage of lifeboats on board *Titanic*.

After informing the captain of the dangers, Andrews immediately set about helping as many people as possible. He dashed from stateroom to stateroom, instructing everyone he could find to put on their life jackets and go up to the deck.

Although an abundance of survivors mentioned seeing Andrews during the sinking, his actions that night were so hurried

Today there is one surviving ship designed by Andrews – the SS Nomadic.

and covered such a vast distance that they are impossible to track. Some passengers reported seeing him throwing deck chairs into the water to be used for flotation devices, others give accounts of him urging passengers onto the lifeboats while some report him heading to the bridge to speak to the captain.

One account of Andrews has entered into legend. A steward, John Stewart, said that he saw Andrews standing alone in the first-class smoking room shortly before the ship sunk. According to Stewart, Andrews was staring at a painting called *Plymouth Harbour*, which depicted the place that *Titanic* was expected to visit on its return voyage. He was standing alone with his life jacket on a nearby table. Although a poignant image, we cannot be sure if this scene actually happened.

However, what we do know from the countless accounts of survivors is that Andrews tirelessly and selflessly attempted to help others at the expense of his own life. One of the stewardesses that Andrews personally saved later commented that: "Mr Andrews met his fate like a true hero, realising the great danger, and gave up his life to save the women and children of the *Titanic*."

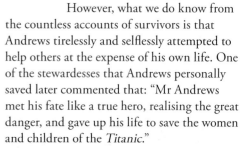

Collapsible boat D was reportedly the last lifeboat to leave Titanic *before it sank.*

As the ship descended into the water, Joughin was positioned at the topmost part.

CHARLES JOUGHIN
HEAD BAKER, 1878-1956

THE BAKER SAVED BY CUNNING, LUCK AND A DOSE OF ALCOHOL

Joughin was no stranger to the sea, having embarked on his first voyage aged 11. He was a skilled cook and became chief baker for many White Star Line steamships, a role he was serving in on *Titanic*'s ill-fated maiden voyage. When the ship struck the iceberg, Joughin was asleep in his bunk. The shock of the impact woke him and he soon learned that lifeboats were preparing to launch. Understanding that passengers would need provisions, he instructed the 13 men working under him to carry four loaves each and load them into the boats.

Understandably shaken, Joughin returned to his cabin and had a quick drink of whisky to calm his nerves. Then, at about 12.30am, he approached the boat he had been assigned, number 10. Joughin helped the women and children onto the lifeboat, but when it was half full, many were hesitant to climb in, believing they were safer on *Titanic* than in the perilous waters of the Atlantic. With the terrified crowd unable to listen to reason, Joughin marched down to the promenade deck, dragged them up the stairs and threw them into the lifeboat. Eventually the boat was close enough to full, but Joughin declined to climb on board, believing the sailors already there would be proficient.

Joughin briefly features as a character in the 1997 Titanic *film, and is seen clinging onto the rail.*

Once the lifeboat had departed, Joughin returned to his quarters and had another drop of liquor. When he re-emerged, all the lifeboats were gone. So Joughin went down to B-Deck and threw deck chairs over the side for flotation devices. After throwing about 50 overboard, he went to the pantry for a drink of water, but heard a loud crash.

Joughin dashed outside and saw crowds of people clambering to get to the poop deck. The ship lurched and threw them into a heap, but Joughin kept his footing. He grabbed the safety rail and positioned himself outside the ship as it went down. As the vessel sank, Joughin rode it down, clutching the rail. His unique position made him the last survivor to leave *Titanic*.

As the ship hit the water, Joughin wasn't pulled down. In fact, he managed to almost step off, barely getting his hair wet. Joughin trod water for two hours until he glimpsed the upturned collapsible boat covered with men. One held his hand as he clung to the side, his legs submerged in the freezing water. He stayed afloat until they were rescued. The only injury he sustained was swollen feet, which many attributed to the alcohol he consumed, believing just the right amount can slow down heat loss.

HOUSE OF COMMONS.

NOTICE given on Thursday, 25th day of April 1912

QUESTION to be put on Monday, 29th day of April 1912

39

※17. Major White,—To ask the President of the Board of Trade, how many navigating officers, exclusive of the captain, were carried in the "Titanic"; what system of officers' watches was carried on board of her; and whether the Board of Trade compel ships to carry navigating officers in some proportion to their tonnage and passenger-carrying capacity. [*Monday 29th April.*]

Mr Buxton,

Seven Navigating Officers, exclusive of the Master, were carried on the "Titanic". I am not able to state what system of watches was adopted. But this question, one within the scope of it relevant, will doubtless be considered by the Court of Inquiry. The Merchant Shipping Acts require that every foreign going ship and every home trade passenger other than a very small vessels ship shall carry a certificated master and also, if of one hundred tons burden or upwards, a certificated mate. If a foreign going ship carries more than one mate, at least the first and second mates must be certificated.

TITANIC ILLUSTRATION

ABOVE: This image appeared on the front cover of an Italian
newspaper reporting on the disaster.

LIFEBOAT LETTER AND BROCHURE

BELOW, RIGHT: Part of a set of correspondence responding to a call by President Taft for ideas on how the great loss of life in shipping tragedies could be prevented in the future. Many letters stated the obvious: proceed more slowly and carefully in areas of ice and pair ships so there would always be a rescue vessel. Those responses with technological innovations range from simplistic and even silly to extensively considered, designed in great detail and already patented.

MATSON LIFE RAFT COMPANY

PRINCIPAL OFFICE
45 MILK STREET .. BOSTON, MASS.

SOLE OWNERS OF PATENTS IN
UNITED STATES
ENGLAND
FRANCE
GERMANY

Apr. 18, 1912.

Secretary Nagel,

    Dept. Commerce & Labor,

    Washington, D.C.

    Dear Sir:--

        The enclosed circular is worth preserving. Had the top hurricane deck of the Steamship Titanic even the rear end, been equipped with ten of these rafts, there is no question but that if everyone on board could not have been saved, the terrible loss of life would have been greatly reduced. We believe in the interest of humanity that this device should be given wide publicity by the press and the general public at large.

        The total monetary loss of the late disaster would have been more than sufficient to supply these rafts on every passenger steamer afloat, both in America and Europe. The expense of equipping the Titanic with these rafts would have been less than $10,000.

        A model of the raft can be seen at the office of the inventor, J. Matson, steward of the Union Club of Boston (#8 Park Street). Previous to the recent disaster, a demonstration of this raft had been ordered by the United States Navy at Washington, to take place at the yards of the Fore River Ship Building Company at Quincy, Mass. -- manufacturers of the rafts.

        This demonstration has been arranged to take place on Saturday the 20th instant, at two o'clock p.m. at the Fore River yards, at Quincy, as above mentioned.

        Regarding the efficiency of these rafts, I further refer you to Mr. Geo. Uhler, Supervising Inspector-General of the Steamboat Inspection Service of the United States.

                      Very truly yours,

                          J. Lewis Price

                        Secretary

JLR/S

The H. J. Matson Life Saving Device

Patented in the United States, France, Great Britain and Germany. Approved by the Department of Commerce and Labor "Steamboat Inspection Service" Oct. 8, 1909.

Adopted by the Compagnie Generale Transatlantique "French Line."

Received from Hon. Gaston Thomson, Secretary of the French Navy, an Official testimony of satisfaction.

Awarded first prize (Large Silver Medal and Diploma) at the *Concours Maritime of Nantes 1908.*

Received the Medal of Honor and Diploma of the "*Societe Nationale d'Encouragement au Bien*" of France.

Awarded the large Bronze Medal of the "*Societe Centrale de Sauvetage des Naufrages*" of France.

Received the Medal of Honor and Diploma of the "*Societe de Hospitaliers Sauveteurs Bretons*" of France.

The above picture taken on board the S. S. "*La Provence*" shows the Matson Life Raft on a Matson Launching Gear for Life Rafts.

Unlike all other life rafts this one is always ready for use; will stand any weather a lifeboat can stand with this difference "It cannot capsize." One man with one pull of the lever of the Matson Launching Gear can launch four life rafts, thus providing in one instant alongside of a burning or sinking ship a life-saving device that will carry 300 people to safety. Each raft has a water tank and a food tank.

No pulleys to get out of order; no ropes to cut; no davits to swing. Will go overboard under any circumstances; will not capsize; will not sink. (It has 12 watertight compartments.) Is built as strong as any lifeboat. Will prevent panic in a moment of danger.

It takes from six to ten men to lower a lifeboat that can carry 40 people. One man can launch four life rafts that will carry 300 people.

The Matson Life Saving Device is considered the best of the epoch by men of high standing in naval affairs who call it "A device admirable in its life saving qualities."

Two Matson Life Rafts were bought and paid for by Charles W. Morse, Esq., which rafts would have been installed on the "Yale" and "Harvard" of the Boston-New York Line, but Mr. Morse's troubles prevented him from taking them from the Custom House in New York and they were sold at auction by the U. S. Government.

In ordering the rafts from the inventor and on being told that they had not yet been approved by the United States Government, Mr. Morse said—"We will put them on as extra as I wish to give our passengers the best of protection."

Testimonials

Les Annales du Bien:
"We wish to congratulate the Compagnie Generale Transatlantique for having put on "La Provence" two Matson Life Rafts, thus showing that nothing is neglected for the safety of her passengers."

Commander Laurent (French Naval Reserve):
"I am convinced that the Matson Life Raft will render great service and I wish to congratulate the inventor."

The New York Marine Journal:
"A great Life Raft, this unique Life Saving Device is the invention of H. J. Matson."

Captain Casabianca (French Navy):
"The Matson Life Raft will be called upon in a moment of disaster to render services that a lifeboat can never render."

Monsieur Bertin (Eminent French Naval Engineer):
"H. J. Matson is to be congratulated for having combined the most practicable Life Saving Device."

The Crew of "La Provence":
"The passengers and crews of ships will ever be grateful to H. J. Matson for having invented such a splendid Life Saving Device."

The Evening Telegram:
"Probably the most unique feature of the S. S. "La Provence" is the Matson Life Raft installed on the ship; hundreds of passengers can be saved by means of new Life Saving Device. The mechanism is so simple and easy of operation that one man can launch a whole fleet of the Life Rafts from a single point in a fraction of a minute.

"We sincerely hope to soon see the Matson Life Raft on all passenger ships so as to avoid the tragic and unrepairable horrors of the sea."

J. Ruaut (Chief Engineer of S. S. La Provence):
"I am convinced that the Matson Life Raft will render great service."

Everybody's Magazine:
"H. J. Matson, Chief Steward of a steamer of the New York and Havre Line, has invented a Life Raft which promises to be useful."

F. Lapleau (Chief Engineer of S. S. La Savoie):
"The Matson Life Raft constitutes the best Life Saving Device of the epoch."

The New York Maritime Register:
"What was apparently the solution of the problem of promptly saving life at sea was demonstrated at the launching of the Matson Life Raft from the deck of Steamship La Savoie at the French Line Pier."

P Tanguy (French Navy):
"Your invention is as ingenious as it is humane and will render immense service in case of shipwreck."

Capt. Jenzequel (Port Officer of Havre):
"Bravo Matson! respectful homage in the name of humanity to the Pasteur of the sea!"

Journal Le Petit Havre:
"The Matson Life Raft is far superior to a lifeboat."

Gloucester Daily Times:
"A slender woman with a touch of her gloved hand pulled a lever which liberated a Matson Life Raft capable of holding fifty-passengers. The raft slid smoothly forward and plunged into the North River; thirty seconds later sailors were at the oars with which the novel craft is provided."

Journal du Havre:
"H. J. Matson searched for a Life-Saving Device that would be rapid, automatic and simultaneous from each side of a ship and he found it."

The Navigazette:
"The Matson Life Raft seems to be the best and most practical Life Saving Device."

The Auto:
"The Matson Life-Saving Device is so simple that it almost makes one wish to be shipwrecked."

Remember the "Slocum"

NOTE:—A working Model of the Matson Life Raft and Launching Device may be seen at the office of the Company,

For further information regarding the Matson Life-Saving Device, interested parties are invited to call upon or address,

Matson Life Raft Company

Room 601, International Trust Co. Bldg., 45 Milk Street, Boston, Mass.

Ch Foraye

THE WHITE HOUSE
APR 21 1912
RECEIVED

OFFICE OF THE SECRETARY
RECEIVED
APR 27 1912
DEPT. OF COMMERCE AND LABOR

Apr 20

Our dear President,
Washington.
D. C.

Please pardon me
for offering a suggestion in
regard to the dreadful disaster
that has just taken place, do
you not think that if they had
lessoned the speed of the Titanic
when they knew they were liable
to come in contact with an Iceberg any moment that they would
have passed it safely even if it

had grazed the ship somewhat.
I would suggest that a law be
passed at once that all vessels
large or small be obliged to
not exceed a certain rate of speed
at any time, and in places of danger that they have no regard to making
time, but use every precaution.
not only to save the passengers.
but also the Ship. Had this
plan been adopted, I doubt very
much if this awful disaster
would have taken place.
You have my sincere
sympathies in the loss of
the Hon. Mr. Butt.

Your very truly,
Your Friend,
One of the late D. L. Moody's
associated Evangelists,
Alexander Skellie.
Cambridge,
Washington Co.
N. Y.

❦ TAFT SUGGESTION LETTER ❦

ABOVE: A letter of 20 April 1912 from the Evangelist
Alexander Skellie to President William H Taft, asking for new
legislation about the speed ships could travel.

E.

Original statement of H. Stone, 2/O.

S.S. "CALIFORNIAN".

At Sea.

5/60   18 Apr. 1912 ?

Captain Lord.

Dear Sir,

At your request I make the following report of the incidents
witnessed by me during my Watch on the Bridge of this Steamer
from mid-night April 14th - 4 a.m. of the 15th.

On going up to the Bridge I was stopped by yourself at the
Wheelhouse Door, and you gave me verbal orders for the Watch.
You showed me a steamer a little abaft our Star-beam and informed
me she was stopped.   You also showed me the loose field ice all
around the ship and a dense Ice-field to the Southward.   You told
me to watch the other steamer and report if she came any nearer
and that you were going to lie down on the Chartroom Settee.   I
went on the Bridge about 8 mins. past 12, and took over the Watch
from the 3rd Off^r, Mr. Groves, who also pointed out ice and
steamer and said our head was E.N.E and we were swinging.   On
looking at the Compass I saw this was correct and observed the
other steamer S.S.E. dead abeam and showing one mast-head light
her red side light and one or two small indistinct lights around
the deck which looked like port-holes or open doors.   I judged
her to be a small tramp steamer and about 5 miles distant.   The
3rd Off^r informed me he had called him up on our Morse Lamp but
had got no reply.   The 3rd Off^r then left the Bridge and I at
once called the steamer up but got no reply.   Gibson, the

ABOVE: The original statement of Second Officer Herbert
Stone of *Californian* about the night of 14/15 April.

E.   - 2 -   18 Apr. 1912 ?

Apprentice, then came up with the Coffee at about 12/15.   I told
him I had called the steamer up and the result.   He then went to
the tapper with the same result.   Gibson thought at first he was
answering, but it was only his mast-head lamps flickering a little.
I then sent Gibson by your orders to get the gear all ready for
streaming a new log line when we got under weigh again.   At 12/35
you whistled up the speaking tube and asked if the other steamer
had moved.   I replied No and that she was on the same bearing and
also reported I had called him up   xxxx the result.   At about
12/45 I observed a flash of light in the sky just above that
steamer.   I thought nothing of it as there were several shooting
stars about the night being firm and clear with light airs and calms.
Shortly after I observed another distinctly over the steamer which
I made out to be a white rocket though observed no flash on the
deck or any indication that it had come from that steamer, in fact
it appeared to come from a good distance beyond her.   Between then
and about 1/15 I observed 3 more the same as before, and all white
in colour.   I, at once, whistled down the speaking tube and you
came from the Chart-room into your own room and answered.   I
reported seeing these lights in the sky in the direction of the
other steamer which appeared to me to be white rockets.   You then
gave me orders to call her up with the Morse Lamp and try and get
some information from her.   You also asked me if they were private
signals and I replied I do not know, but they were all white.   You
then said,"when you get an answer let me know by Gibson".   Gibson
and I observed 3 more at intervals and kept calling them up on our
Morse Lamps but got no reply whatsoever.   The other steamer mean-

while had shut in her red side light and showed us her stern light and her mast-head's glow was just visible. I observed the steamer to be steaming away to the S.W. and altering her bearing fast. We were also swinging slowly all the time through S. and at 1/50 were heading about W.S.W. and the other steamer bearing S.W. x W. At 2 a.m. the vessel was steaming away fast and only just her stern light was visible and bearing S.W.½ W. I sent Gibson down to you and told him to wake you and tell you we had seen altogether 8 white rockets and that the steamer had gone out of sight to the S.W. Also that we were heading W.S.W. When he came back he reported he had told you we had called him up repeatedly and got no answer, and you replied "All right", are you sure there were no colours in them, and Gibson replied, No they were all white. At 2/45 I again whistled down again and told you we had seen no more lights and that the steamer had steamed away to the S.W. and was now out of sight, also that the rockets were all white and had no colours whatever.

We saw nothing further until about 3/20 when we thought we observed two faint lights in the sky about S.S.W. and a little distance apart. At 3/40 I sent Gibson down to see all was ready for me to prepare the new log at 8 bells. The Chief Off^r, Mr. Stewart, came on the Bridge at 4 a.m. and I gave him a full report of what I had seen and my reports and replies from you, and pointed out where I thought I had observed these faint lights at 3/20. He picked up the Binoculars and said after a few moments "There she is then, she's all right, she is a four master". I said "Then that isn't the steamer I saw first", took up the glasses and just made

out a four masted steamer with two mast-head lights a little abaft our port beam, and bearing about S., we were heading about W.N.W.

Mr. Stewart then took over the Watch and I went off the Bridge

Yours respectfully,

(sgd). Herbert Stone.

2nd Officer.

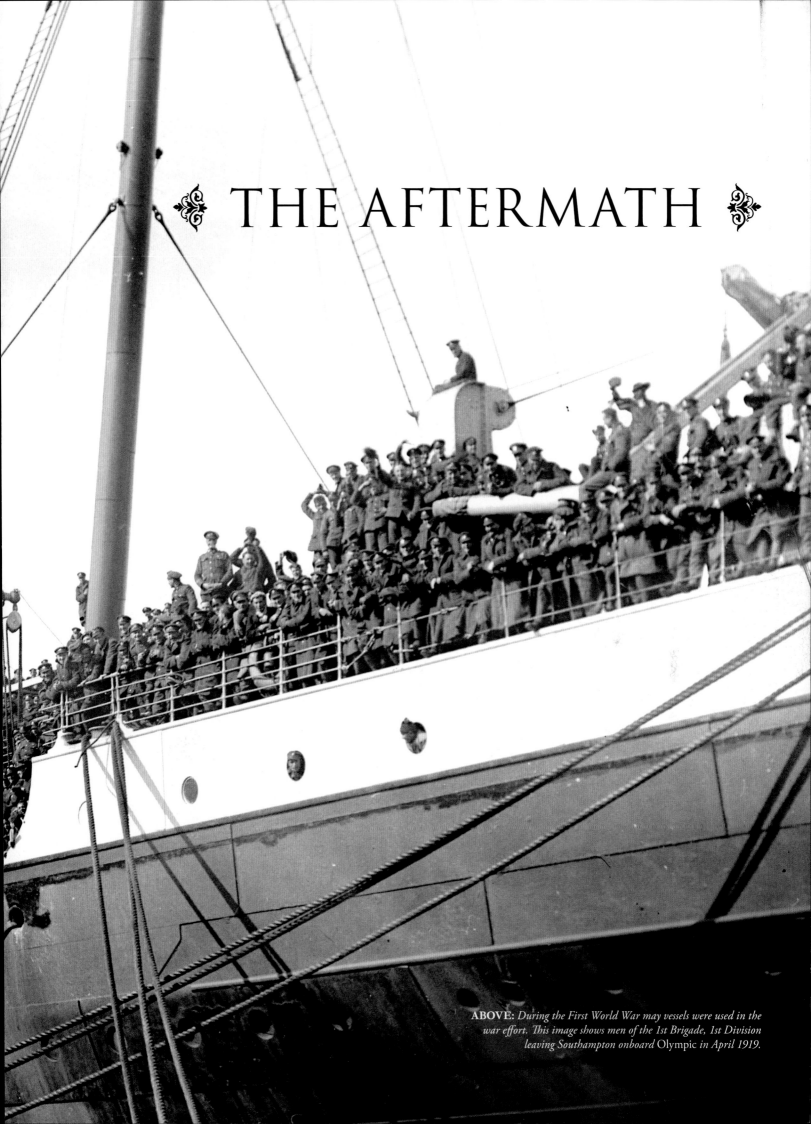

❧ THE AFTERMATH ❧

ABOVE: *During the First World War may vessels were used in the war effort. This image shows men of the 1st Brigade, 1st Division leaving Southampton onboard* Olympic *in April 1919.*

COVERING AN INTERNATIONAL SENSATION

T he loss of *Titanic* was one of the greatest news events of all time. Well before the survivors were even rescued, rumours about it had flashed over the wireless throughout the world. By the time Harold Cottam and Harold Bride began transmitting the list of survivors (information not immediately made available to the public), most newspaper editors had already made the assessment that any damage to the "unsinkable ship" would be an inconvenience rather than a tragedy. *The Daily Mirror* of London, for example, produced a headline stating "EVERYONE SAFE", while proclaiming "Helpless Giant Being Towed to Port by Allan Liner".

One newspaper, however, did not make such assumptions. It was 1:20am on 15 April when a bulletin reporting that *Titanic* had struck an iceberg and was sinking at the bow reached the newsroom of *The New York Times*. Carr Van Anda, the managing editor, immediately made calls to correspondents in Halifax, a wireless station in Montreal that had received the news via the steamer *Virginian*, and officials of the White Star Line. The last had not received an update since the first wireless report. Unlike other editors, Van Anda reasoned that the terrible silence meant only

INTERVIEWING HAROLD BRIDE

Van Anda's greatest coup was gaining an exclusive interview with Harold Bride. Wireless inventor Guglielmo Marconi planned to speak to Bride and Harold Cottam; Van Anda, who was Marconi's good friend, persuaded him to do it aboard *Carpathia* and to take *The New York Times* reporter Jim Speers with him. Backed by a little bluster, Speers was able to board the ship with Marconi long before any other reporters. At Marconi's request, Bride gave Speers an extended account of the disaster. The next day it appeared verbatim over five columns of the front page, and it is still considered one of the most gripping stories in newspaper history.

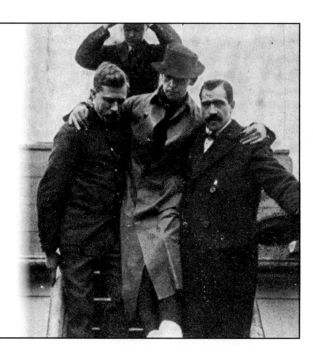

ABOVE: *Harold Bride was carried off* Carpathia *in New York as his feet were too badly frozen for him to walk. Despite his injuries, he spent most of* Carpathia's *voyage helping Harold Cottam in the wireless room.*

one thing: it had not been possible to send more messages. He immediately reorganized the first page of the late edition, with articles about the famous people aboard, previous times ships had collided with icebergs, other vessels that had reported ice in the region, and, in a bold box, the latest news as it had come through on the wireless.

When the paper went to press at 3:30am, not only did it give more background than any other newspaper, it was the only major daily newspaper to report flatly that *Titanic* had gone down. By the next day, businessmen, families of those aboard *Titanic* and the curious public all crowded outside newspaper offices, Lloyd's at the Royal Exchange and White Star's headquarters in London, Southampton and New York, waiting for information.

Many of the newspapers being sold on the streets still claimed that all the passengers had been saved. But the headline of *The New York Times* stated: "TITANIC SINKS FOUR HOURS AFTER HITTING ICEBERG; 866 RESCUED BY CARPATHIA, PROBABLY 1250 PERISH; ISMAY SAFE, MRS. ASTOR MAYBE, NOTED NAMES MISSING". By 17 April, the thorough coverage by Van Anda's team had led to newspapers around the world lifting their material straight from *The New York Times*.

But Van Anda's greatest success was still to come. With *Carpathia* scheduled to arrive at 9:30pm on 18 April, this gave him only three

CARR VAN ANDA

The coverage of the *Titanic* disaster was only one of many triumphs for Carr Van Anda, who is often considered the greatest managing editor in American journalistic history. Van Anda left Ohio University after only two years to become a journalist. He worked for progressively prestigious newspapers until, at age just 28, he became night editor of *The Sun* in New York. In 1904 he was hired by Adolph Ochs to rejuvenate the newsroom of *The New York Times*, and he subsequently built it into the finest news-gathering organization in the United States.

ABOVE LEFT: *For several days after* Titanic's *demise, huge crowds constantly swarmed around the White Star Line offices in New York, London and Southampton hoping for news – which proved to be distressing more often than not.*

ABOVE RIGHT: *The front page of* The Daily Mirror *on 16 April 1912. After initially reporting that everyone was safe, it, like other papers, backtracked to acknowledge the disaster that had occurred.*

hours to cover the biggest story in the world before the first edition went to press at 12:30am. He hired an entire floor of a hotel near Cunard's pier, fully staffed it with editors and installed four telephone lines directly to the rewrite desk of *The New York Times*. He also sent 16 reporters to cover every aspect of the story, although it had already been determined that no newspaper could have more than four passes to the pier and no one would be allowed on the ship until all survivors had left. The reporters and accompanying photographers were assigned in advance to almost every imaginable angle of the story.

Van Anda's careful organization paid off. Friday morning's first edition contained 15 pages (out of 24) about *Titanic*, including an interview with Bride that was the journalistic highlight of the entire tragedy. Almost a century later that edition is still considered a masterpiece of newspaper history. More importantly, *The New York Times* coverage of the disaster helped greatly to secure the reputation and financial position of a newspaper that had been struggling, and to establish it as one of the world's key centres of journalistic innovation and excellence. Years later, when Van Anda was visiting the British press baron Lord Northcliffe, his host pulled a copy of *The New York Times* from 19 April 1912 out of his desk. "We keep this", he said, "as an example of the greatest accomplishment in news reporting".

66 **The terrible news of the sinking of the *Titanic* reached New York at about eleven o'clock last night and the scene on Broadway was awful. Crowds of people were coming out of the theatres, cafés were going full tilt, and autos whizzing everywhere, when the newsboys began to cry 'Extra! Extra Paper! *Titanic* sunk with 1,800 on board!' ... Nobody could realize what had happened, and when they did begin to understand, the excitement was almost enough to cause a panic in the theatres. ... The scene in front of the steamship office was a tragedy in itself.** 99

– Alexander Macomb

ABOVE: *Hundreds of family members and well-wishers descended on the Southampton train station on 29 April as the crew, most of whom were from the Southampton area, arrived home by train from Plymouth.*

RIGHT: *Newsboy Ned Parfett has a bustling trade selling newspapers on 16 April outside the White Star Line offices at Oceanic House on Cockspur Street in London.*

THE OFFICIAL INQUIRIES

At 10:30am on 19 April, little more than 12 hours after *Carpathia* reached New York, a US Senate investigation into the disaster officially opened. It has been argued that it was convened to establish responsibility; to prove negligence, therefore providing American passengers with the right to sue *Titanic*'s owners; or to force the enactment of new maritime legislation. Regardless, it quickly became a personal forum for the inquiry's chairman, Michigan Senator William Alden Smith. In 17 days of testimony over five weeks, Smith used his position as chairman to dominate the questioning, despite showing a remarkable ignorance of ships and navigation.

The first of 82 witnesses was J Bruce Ismay, who was interrogated about the ship's speed, the damage incurred from the ice and how he obtained a place in a lifeboat. Other witnesses included the four surviving officers, wireless operator Harold Bride, wireless inventor Guglielmo Marconi, 34 crew members and 21 passengers. Captain Stanley Lord and two men from the ship *Californian* were also questioned; they told of a mysterious ship that fired a number of rockets before, after failing to respond to signals, simply disappearing. Significantly, Smith did not interview a single officer who had been on the bridge of *Californian* on the night of 14/15

LEFT: *The US Senate inquiry was played out before a standing-room-only audience day after day. Here, Third Officer Herbert Pittman is being questioned.*

ABOVE: *Guglielmo Marconi, the inventor of the wireless and the 1909 Nobel Prize winner in Physics, testified at both inquiries regarding the use of the wireless for safety and general communications at sea.*

> **Q. Did Third Class passengers have same chance as others to reach safety?**
>
> Just shortly after the Swedish girl and I got above, by using the emergency stairway, the main stairway doors were opened and those below could then get up. Until then there was no help of any kind accorded to Third Class passengers. So, it was only in the very last desperate moments that Third Class passengers were given any chance to reach safety.
>
> – *Anna Kincaid*

 ## LIGHTOLLER ON THE STAND

One of the most impressive performances during the inquiries was by Second Officer Charles Lightoller. Questions posed in both countries tried to show that the White Star Line – via its captain and senior officers – had been negligent, and should therefore be liable for damages. However, Lightoller proved extremely able at protecting White Star and avoiding any admission harmful to his former colleagues. He emphasized the unusual weather conditions and claimed that no ship's captain reduced speed under such a situation. His testimony helped both White Star and Captain Smith to escape without significant blame.

TOP: *Sir Cosmo Duff Gordon received intensive – and rather confrontational – interrogation during the British Board of Trade inquiry, particularly from W D Harbinson, the counsel for the steerage passengers.*

ABOVE LEFT: *Bruce Ismay (with moustache) was the first witness called at the US Senate inquiry. He was questioned primarily about the ship's speed in areas of ice and about his own boarding of Collapsible C.*

THE ORDEAL OF SIR COSMO DUFF GORDON

Perhaps the most publicized sideshow of the British inquiry was the testimony of Sir Cosmo Duff Gordon. He was questioned extensively about his offer of £5 to each of the crew aboard Lifeboat 1, which was viewed by many as a bribe so they would not return to rescue those in the water. Clearly none of the interrogating barristers believed him when he denied hearing any suggestions about going back. Lady Duff Gordon's subsequent testimony did not help her husband's credibility, and although Sir Cosmo received no official censure, his public reputation was ruined.

April. By the end of the hearings, testimony and affidavits filled 1,145 pages.

In his report, Senator Smith rebuked the British Board of Trade for not requiring enough lifeboats, criticized Captain Smith for his lack of precautions in an area of ice, praised Captain Rostron and denounced Captain Lord for failing to aid *Titanic*. Smith concluded that *Californian* was far closer to *Titanic* than the 30.5 kilometres (19 miles) reported by Lord, saw her distress signals and failed to come to her rescue, initiating a controversy that continues today. Smith also made several significant recommendations: that it become mandatory for ships to carry lifeboats with a total capacity to hold each person aboard; that lifeboat drills be instituted for crew and passengers and that wireless equipment be manned 24 hours per day.

Before the American investigation was even finished, the British Board of Trade initiated its own Court of Inquiry, with 72-year-old Lord Mersey serving as commissioner, and Attorney General Sir Rufus Isaacs as counsel to the Board of Trade. Officially, there were 26 topics – including issues of construction, *Titanic*'s speed, ice warnings received, number of lifeboats and behaviour of the crew and passengers – for which the inquiry was attempting to gain information and find answers. But although there were ultimately 96 witnesses =and 25,622 questions

and answers – many believe that from the start, Mersey had an agenda: to whitewash any negligence by the Board of Trade and the White Star Line, and to find a culprit to whom he could attach blame.

The inquiry was wide-ranging in those questioned, from the crew to Marconi to Antarctic explorer Sir Ernest Shackleton, but it generally followed the issues raised in the American inquiry. Under the circumstances, Mersey's conclusions were totally predictable. Both Ismay and Sir Cosmo Duff Gordon were exonerated. No blame was found in the treatment of third-class passengers. Although it was ruled *Titanic* was going too fast, Captain Smith was cleared of negligence. Both the Board of Trade, which had let *Titanic* sail without the necessary lifeboats, and the White Star Line were absolved of any significant fault, meaning that their financial liability was limited.

But there was still a need for a scapegoat and, having long had his mind made up in this regard, Lord Mersey easily found one. He held that *Californian* had been the "mystery ship", as close as eight kilometres (five miles) away, and that she could have easily reached *Titanic* but had not made the effort. Thus, it was not the lack of lifeboats, excessive speed or even the iceberg responsible for the tragedy; it was the officers of *Californian*, and most notably, Captain Lord.

❝ They cried out, 'Any more women,' saw us, & came to try & drag Madame & I away from Sir Cosmo, but Madame clung to Sir Cosmo, & begged him not to let them take her, or separate her, she said, I will go down with you, and I clung to Madame, I would not leave them, it would have been too awful to have been alone. After all the lifeboats had gone, everybody seemed to rush to the other side of the boat, & leave ours vacant, but we still stood there, as Sir Cosmo said, we must wait for orders, presently an officer started to swing off a little boat called the 'Emergency' boat, quite an ordinary little rowing boat & started to man it, he saw us & ordered us in, they were then firing the rockets beside us, we had to be nearly thrown up into this boat, two other American gentlemen jumped in, & seven stokers, they started to lower us.**❞**

– Laura Mable Francatelli

❝ Mr. Carter and I did not get into the boat until after they had begun to lower it away. When the boat reached the water I helped to row it, pushing the oar from me as I sat. This is the explanation of the fact that my back was to the sinking steamer. The boat would have accommodated certainly six or more passengers in addition if there had been any on the boat deck to go. These facts can be substantiated by Mr. E.E. Carter, of Philadelphia, who got in at the time that I did and was rowing the boat with me. I hope I need not say that neither Mr. Carter nor myself would for one moment have thought of getting into the boat if there had been any women to go in it…**❞**

– Bruce Ismay

ABOVE: *Sir Cosmo Duff Gordon, whose reputation was ruined by the charges that he had offered each of the sailors in Lifeboat 1 £5 in order not to return to the scene of the carnage when* Titanic *sank.*

CALIFORNIAN AND THE MYSTERY SHIP

For decades, Captain Stanley Lord of *Californian* has been cast as the villain of the *Titanic* disaster for failing to respond to her distress signals. Ever since the official inquiries determined that the two ships were closer to each other than Lord stated, many have assumed that *Titanic*'s "mystery ship" was *Californian*. But putting aside the desire to find a culprit, what do the facts actually indicate?

A cargo vessel of 6,223 tons, *Californian* left Liverpool for Boston on 5 April. On the night of 14 April, surrounded by loose ice, *Californian* stopped at a position calculated as 42°05'North, 50°07'West, 35 kilometres (22 miles) north of the remains of *Titanic*. At about 11pm, Lord saw the lights of what he considered a small steamer, and asked wireless operator Cyril Evans which other ships were nearby. Evans only knew of *Titanic*, but the ship Lord saw was far too small for that. Nevertheless, Lord ordered Evans to contact *Titanic* about the ice; he was promptly cut off by Jack Phillips.

By 11:30pm, the ship's green starboard light was visible about eight kilometres (five miles) away, but Third Officer Charles Groves was unable to make contact by Morse lamp. When Second Officer Herbert Stone replaced Groves on watch at midnight, he ordered apprentice James Gibson to continue Morsing the ship. Then, at 12:40am, a series of rockets began to shoot through the mysterious ship's rigging. In the

next hour, eight rockets appeared, which puzzled Stone, because the ship began to steam away, which was unexpected from a ship in distress. At about 2:20am she disappeared. Stone sent Gibson to inform the captain, who was sleeping, but Lord later stated that, perhaps because he was exhausted, he could not remember being given such information.

Around 5:00am, going onto deck, Lord saw a ship about 13 kilometres (eight miles) away. He ordered Evans to contact her, and when the operator turned on the wireless, he heard about *Titanic*. Lord immediately headed to the coordinates that had been transmitted from the doomed ship, where he found the steamer Mount Temple, but nothing else. Continuing on, he met *Carpathia* and continued the search for survivors.

Lord testified in the US hearings, but found that sensational newspaper reports of statements by crewman Ernest Gill had already influenced Senator Smith. Smith's negative position was bolstered by Captain John Knapp of the US

 ## THE TREACHERY OF ERNEST GILL

Ernest Gill was a crewman who deserted after *Californian* arrived in Boston. For almost two years' wages, he sold to the press a sensational and clearly fabricated story about a vessel he could see in distress at the time the rockets were fired. Because of this tale, Gill was one of three men from *Californian* to appear before the US Senate inquiry, where his testimony was inconsistent and at odds with other accounts and reports. Nevertheless, it allowed Smith's search for a scapegoat to focus upon Captain Lord, who paid the price for Gill's avaricious scheme.

TOP RIGHT: *The SS* Mount Temple. *When* Californian *arrived at the coordinates Jack Phillips had broadcast, all they found was* Mount Temple *under Captain James Henry Moore.*

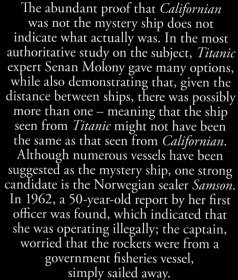

WHAT WAS THE MYSTERY SHIP?

The abundant proof that *Californian* was not the mystery ship does not indicate what actually was. In the most authoritative study on the subject, *Titanic* expert Senan Molony gave many options, while also demonstrating that, given the distance between ships, there was possibly more than one – meaning that the ship seen from *Titanic* might not have been the same as that seen from *Californian*. Although numerous vessels have been suggested as the mystery ship, one strong candidate is the Norwegian sealer *Samson*. In 1962, a 50-year-old report by her first officer was found, which indicated that she was operating illegally; the captain, worried that the rockets were from a government fisheries vessel, simply sailed away.

❝ **Many questions will for ever remain unanswered concerning the failure of *Californian* to render assistance to the stricken ship. Mr. Stone knew without a shadow of doubt that there was trouble aboard the vessel from which the distress signals had been fired but he failed to convince his Captain; but did Captain Lord need any convincing? Was Mr. Stone afraid that if he was too insistent he would arouse the wrath of his superior? Why did Captain Lord take no efficient steps to render assistance before 6 o'clock?**

Did he consider problematical damage to his ship was of more importance than the saving of lives? ❞ — *Charles Groves*

Navy, who created a map showing positions he attributed to *Titanic* and *Californian* and "proving" they were seen by each other. These positions were highly inaccurate, but helped produce Smith's condemnation of Lord.

The British inquiry followed the Senate's lead, despite numerous major discrepancies, including that the sound of *Titanic*'s rockets would have been audible to any vessel in sight, that both *Titanic* and *Californian* were stationary but the mystery ship was moving, and that a ship the size of *Titanic* would be unmistakable at close range. Lord Mersey

chose to ignore any data or testimony in favour of his pre-determined scapegoat, and, as Lord was called only as a witness, with no charges against him, he was unable to defend himself. Lord's reputation was ruined, and he was soon forced to resign from the Leyland Line. Despite later efforts, he died in 1962 without clearing his name.

The discovery of *Titanic* in 1985 in a location significantly different than that Phillips transmitted was further proof that *Californian* was not the mystery ship, and that she could not have reached *Titanic* in time to

save the passengers even if Lord had steamed towards the disaster area immediately after the rockets had been seen.

Seven years later, the first official vindication of Lord was produced, when a Department of Transport investigation determined that *Californian* was 27–32 kilometres (17–20 miles) away and out of sight of the sinking liner. The final report indicated that the officers of *Californian* had indeed seen the rockets of *Titanic* through the rigging, but that any fault in failing to act lay with Second Officer Stone.

ABOVE: *Crew of* Californian *summoned to give evidence at the British inquiry. Among those pictured are wireless operator Cyril Evans, apprentice James Gibson and Second Officer Herbert Stone (third, fourth and fifth from left).*

AFTER THE TRAGEDY

I t was 1913, and "Craganour", owned by Charles Bower Ismay, had just won the Derby at Epsom. The signal "Winner All Right" had been given so that payments on bets could be made, and the horse had been taken to the Winner's Circle. Suddenly the stewards, despite no official complaint having been registered, announced that "Craganour" had jostled several other horses and that they had awarded the victory to "Aboyeur". Was the rumour true – that the racing establishment would never let a horse owned by an Ismay win the Derby? No one really knows, but the story adds a twist to one definite fact: that the sinking of *Titanic* not only changed forever the lives of many who survived the tragedy, but also of others only tangentially involved, such as J Bruce Ismay's younger brother.

Despite the lack of censure by the British board of inquiry, Ismay himself was never to escape public disapproval for living when so many others died. The same was true of Cosmo Duff Gordon, who lived with allegations about his lack of bravery until his death in 1931, six years before Ismay. Sadly, the same blame attached to other men who had survived, including Major Arthur Peuchen, Dickinson Bishop (who was the subject of unfounded rumours of having entered a boat dressed as a woman) and the ship's officers, none of whom ever gained promotion to captain in the merchant fleet.

Conversely, the events gained fame for some of the players in the tragedy. Arthur Rostron was awarded the Congressional Medal of Honor and the American Cross of Honor and went on to command *Caronia*, *Lusitania* and *Mauretania*. He was knighted in 1926. Margaret "Molly" Brown's heroism and care for others aboard *Titanic*, in Lifeboat 6 and on *Carpathia*, made her a national figure, and she was immortalized in the Broadway musical, later to become a feature film, *The Unsinkable Molly Brown*.

Although some survivors found it easy to rebuild their lives, others did not. Charlotte Cardeza, who had occupied the most expensive cabin on the ship, seemed most concerned about replacing the 14 trunks, four suitcases and three crates of baggage she and her son had brought aboard. She filed the largest claim against the White Star Line, seeking $177,352.75 for her losses. Marion Wright,

ABOVE: *The body of a victim is recovered from the ocean. So many bodies were recovered that the cable-ship* Mackay-Bennett *was nicknamed the "Funeral Ship".*

RIGHT: *Passengers boarding the luxury train "The Capitol" at Washington Union station, bound for Chicago. A brightly lit marquee announces that the movie that will be screened during the journey is* The Unsinkable Molly Brown.

THE TITANIC GRAVEYARDS

After the remains of 59 victims of the disaster were claimed, 150 bodies remained in Halifax. Their burials began on 3 May, and many people attended to honour those being interred so far from home. The *Titanic* plot at Mount Olivet Cemetery was intended for Catholics, and 19 individuals were buried there. The plot at Baron De Hirsch Cemetery, which received ten bodies, was intended for Jewish victims, but some were buried elsewhere, and Michel Navratil was mistakenly interred there because he had used the alias Hoffman. The other 121 victims, initially presumed to be Protestants, were placed in Fairview Lawn Cemetery.

who had sung a solo at the second-class hymn-sing on the evening of the collision, was met by her fiancé in New York, where the two were married that week. They moved to a farm in Oregon, where they lived together for 49 years. Dr Washington Dodge survived with his wife and son, but suffered a mental breakdown in 1919 and committed suicide. Second-class passenger Edwina Trout suffered emotional problems for months, but recovered and eventually moved to California. There she outlived three successive husbands and became a popular figure at *Titanic* events, dying in 1984 at the age of 100.

Eleanor Widener, Emily Ryerson and Madeleine Astor all later remarried, Madeleine thus relinquishing all claim to the Astor fortune. Their previous families were not forgotten, however. In August 1912, Madeleine gave birth to a son, whom she named John Jacob Astor V. The body

of her late husband had been one of the most easily identifiable of those found by *Mackay-Bennett*, his initials discovered in his shirt collar and his effects including a gold watch, gold and diamond cufflinks, a diamond ring and $2,440 cash. Eleanor Widener chose to commemorate her son lost on *Titanic* with a $3.5 million donation to build the Harry Elkins Widener Memorial Library, the primary building of the Harvard University library system.

Finally, two of the key ships in the *Titanic* story suffered similar fates. In November 1915, *Californian* was torpedoed by an enemy submarine in the Mediterranean. She sank, but only one man was lost. In July 1918, *Carpathia* was crossing from Liverpool to Boston when she was also torpedoed – three times in total. She took two and a half hours to sink, and all but five of the 280 aboard were rescued.

ABOVE LEFT: *A memorial in Halifax to those lost. There are three separate graveyards in Halifax where victims are buried.*

ABOVE RIGHT: *A Congressional Medal of Honor, like the one awarded to Rostron.*

❝ Everybody says that I don't look much like anyone who has been through such a terrible experience…Everything was so sudden & my heart is full of thankfulness to God for having preserved me through all the great kindness shown by quite strangers right along from New York, still continues. We have about 20 fresh presents including doz silver spoons, silver cruet stand, a beautifully bound teacher's bible, prayer & hymn book, picture, damask table cloth, doz dinner napkins, a quart jug from a neighbour; 4 or 5 under garments for myself, £2 from a friend of Arthur's in Chicago, & about doz songs from various people…❞

– Marion Wright

WHAT HAPPENED TO OLYMPIC AND BRITANNIC?

Titanic was not the only one of White Star's three giant ships to meet an early demise. The third was originally to be named *Gigantic* but was launched in 1914 as *Britannic*. Serving as a hospital ship in the First World War, she either struck a mine or was torpedoed in 1916 in the Aegean, and sank within an hour. *Olympic*, on the other hand, had a long career after being given a refit to increase her lifeboat capacity, raise her bulkheads and build a new inner skin. She spent much of the Great War as a naval transport ship, but then returned to regular service, making hundreds of Atlantic crossings before being retired in 1935, after which she was stripped of her fittings and scrapped.

❝ My husband was such a loving man and Father. I have a little boy 13 nearly overcome with grief he has gone to a new school a Mr. Taylor's in Freshfield, he has promised to look after him, and to try to comfort him. We have taken a small house here for a year, our old home was too painful to stay in. How my husband loved his work at the office, and you for your kindness to him – he was so proud of his position as Private help to you.

I hope you will be able to do something for us, we should love to keep our home, so that we can keep together although very lonely. ❞

– Anne Harrison

❝ My life would have been over if you had not been saved. For me there never has been & never could be any man but you & I feel I can never express the gratitude & thankfulness that fills me for your escape. Only a week ago today that I watched that magnificent vessel sail away so proudly. I never dreamt of danger as I wished her God speed. I have wished many times since Monday night that I had gone with you, I might have helped you in this awful hour. I know so well what bitterness of spirit you must be feeling for the loss of so many precious lives & the ship itself that you loved like a living thing. ❞

– Florence Bruce Ismay

ABOVE: Olympic, *the sister ship of* Titanic. *Of the three great ships envisioned in 1907 by J Bruce Ismay and Lord Pirrie, she was the only one to lead a full life, finally being retired in 1935.*

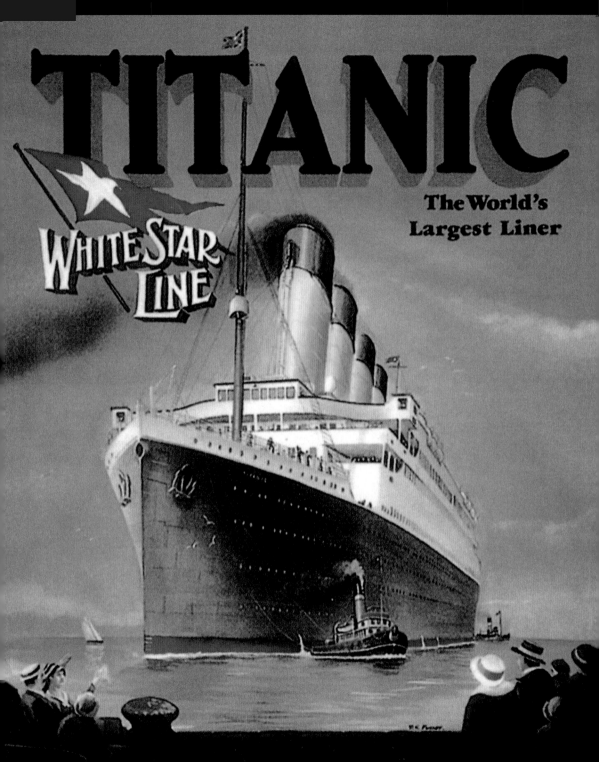

TITANIC

The World's Largest Liner

WHITE STAR LINE

SOUTHAMPTON ~ NEW YORK

VIA CHERBOURG & QUEENSTOWN

❖ TITANIC POSTER 1912 ❖

ABOVE: One of the original posters issued by White Star Line to

DEBBIE REYNOLDS

BELOW: Debbie Reynolds as the title character in the 1964 film *The Unsinkable Molly Brown*.

❖ CLAIM FORM ❖

BELOW: The forms sent by the Board of Trade to the father of Ernest Price, a 17-year-old barman in *Titanic*'s à la Carte restaurant. The forms deal with his still-to-be-paid wages and the return of the personal effects found on his body when it was recovered. Also included is the envelope in which the forms were sent.

W. & E. 1. No. 618
12/13

Port of SOUTHAMPTON.

Account of Wages and Effects of a Deceased Seaman

ISSUED BY THE
BOARD OF TRADE

* Name of Ship.	Official Number.	Port of Registry.	Name of Master.	Description of Voyage or Employment.
"TITANIC."	131428.	Liverpool.	E. J. Smith.	New York.

Name of Seaman.	Rating.	* Date of Engagement.	Date of Death.	Place of Death.	Cause of Death.
Rice Ernest Eugn Barma		20th April.	15th April.	Lat. 41. 16 N. Long. 50. 14 W.	Drowning.

* If the Seaman's name is not on the Articles, in this space must be entered the date of his being sent on board the ship; and in such case here state by whom and where he was sent on board, *and any other particulars.*

‡ If the man is in debt to the Ship, the word "nil" must be entered in the money column.

Wages, Money, Clothes, and other Effects.	Amount.	Inventory, copied from the Official Log Book, of Articles sold, and the Sum received for each.	Amount for each Article sold.	Deductions. *Notice to Masters.—*For all deductions made, reasons must be given to the satisfaction of the Superintendent; and when possible, they should be proved by receipts or entries in the Official Log Book."		Initials of Superintendent against each Item checked.
				Particulars of Deductions. †	Amount.	
Wages, at £ 1 1 1 per Month Months. 6 Days.						
Deductions as per Account						
‡ Balance of Wages due to Seaman						
Money in possession of Deceased						
Proceeds of Sale of Clothes and other Effects, as per Account						
				Total		
Net Amount... nil		✓ Inventory of Articles unsold, see Endorsement.			Total	

MAY 1912
G. R. & R. O.

If satisfactory evidence is not produced in justification of the deductions, the Superintendent should withhold clearance, and refer the case for the decision of the Board of Trade.

I HEREBY declare that the above is a true and correct account of the Money, Wages, and Effects of the above-named Deceased Seaman.
Dated this 7 day of May 19 12 For WHITE STAR LINE.
{ Signature of the Master of the Vessel. }

The particulars respecting the deceased in the following columns are to be filled up if, and so far as, the Master is acquainted with them; and if any Will has been deposited with the Master, it must be given to the Superintendent.

Birth-place.	Age.	If any Will has been made, Name and Address of Executor.	Married or Single.	If Married, the Name and Residence of his Wife.	If any Children, their Names and Ages.	Name and Residence of Father and Mother, or of the nearest known relation.
Ldn	14					93 Grove Rd Holloway London

I HEREBY certify that I have examined the above account, and compared the Inventory with the Official Log Book, which is attested by the Mate and one of the Crew, and that the above is a true copy thereof. The Balance of the Account has been paid to me, and the unsold articles have been delivered at this Office,

this 7 day of May 19 12

Superintendent.

I certify that the above has been compared with the List *&c.* and that the Account is correct.
this 17th day of May 19 12
Registrar General.

(See Endorsement.)

* Prefix "S.S." if a steam ship.

(156.) (64299) Wt. 3610½ 25 5000 2-11 W B & L

[P.T.O.

Whenever any Seaman or Apprentice belonging to or sent home in any British ship, whether a foreign-going ship or a home-trade ship employed on a voyage which is to terminate in the United Kingdom, dies during such Voyage, the Master must take charge of all money, clothes and effects which he leaves on board, and shall, if he thinks fit, cause all or any of the said clothes and effects to be sold by auction at the mast or other public auction, and must thereupon sign an entry in the Official Log Book containing a statement of the amount of the money and a description of the effects so left by the deceased; in case of a sale, a description of each article sold, and the sum received for each; and a statement of the sum due to the deceased as wages, and the total amount of the deductions (if any) to be made from such wages; and must cause such entry to be attested by a Mate and by one of the Crew. The Monies so received and taken charge of, together with any effects that may remain unsold, and the balance of wages due to the deceased, must be delivered by the Master to the Superintendent of a Mercantile Marine Office, in the case of a foreign-going ship, when he attends before that Officer, to discharge his Crew; and in the case of a home-trade ship, upon his first arrival in any port after the death has occurred. Any Master who makes default is liable, in addition to the above payments, to a penalty not exceeding treble the amount unaccounted for, or not exceeding £50.

Every Master is bound, under like penalties, to deliver an account to the Superintendent of such effects, money, and wages, and for this purpose the above-mentioned particulars in this form must be all fully and correctly filled up.

Inventory of Articles unsold belonging to the within mentioned deceased Seaman, delivered to the Superintendent.

Comb.
Knife.
2 bottle openers.
Letters.

The above-mentioned articles are contained in* one canvas bag No. 186.

under Company's seal

Order (W. & E. 6) issued
-9 JUL 1912

* Here state **Number** and **Description** of Packages.

❧ TAFT SUGGESTION LETTER ❧

BELOW: A letter of 20 April 1912 from the Evangelist Alexander Skellie to President William H Taft, asking for new legislation about the speed ships could travel.

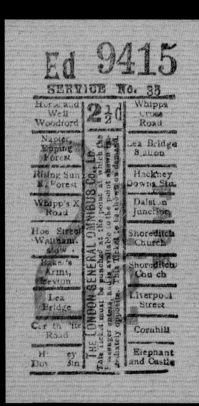

❧ BUS TICKET ❧

ABOVE: A remarkably well-preserved bus ticket that was recovered from the wreck of *Titanic*.

DUPLICATE.

FROM WHITE STAR LINE,

ROYAL MAIL HOUSE,

LEADENHALL STREET,

LONDON, E.C.3.

PASSENGER TRAFFIC & CONFERENCE DEPARTMENT

FOR........E. J. Foley, Esq.
                Board of Trade,
                London, S.W.1.

............9th December............19 29.

Dear Sir Haldane,

"ATLANTIC" FILM.

You may recall that you were kind enough some few
months ago to personally intervene with the Director of the
Elstree Film Studio in connection with the "Atlantic" Film then
under production; and with the view to their dropping their
project, as we felt at the time that the production could be
regarded only as contrary to the interests of British shipping.

Your friend the Director at Elstree pointed out that
matters had gone too far but that there would in any case be no
direct reference either to the White Star Line or to the "Titanic".

As you will probably know, this film is now being
featured all over England, and it is understood that they have
actually taken the Alhambra Theatre for showing this film over
Christmas.

The worst feature, however, is that I find in
Germany from which country I have just returned, that this film is
being featured at all the leading cinemas where naturally they

N O T I C E

The Producers desire to assure the Public that

the incidents depicted are not such as are likely to

occur in the present day, as it is the practice of all

Shipping Companies and a requirement of the Board of

Trade, to provide

BOATS FOR ALL

THE LEGACY OF TITANIC

LEFT: *Researchers from one of the earliest dives to locate Titanic in 1986 struggle to get their submersible out of the Atlantic Ocean.*

SEARCH AND DISCOVERY

T he dream of finding, or even raising, *Titanic* is virtually as old as the tragedy itself. Shortly after the disaster, several wealthy families – the Astors, Guggenheims and Wideners – proposed that the Merritt and Chapman Derrick and Wrecking Company conduct a salvage operation for the ship, but the technical limitations of the time simply did not allow such a venture to go ahead. In the following half-century, a succession of schemes was proposed, most of them totally impractical.

In 1980, the first serious attempt to locate the ship was launched. Flamboyant Texas oil millionaire Jack Grimm and film producer Mike Harris led an expedition on the research vessel *H J W Fay* to find *Titanic* using side-scan sonar. Grimm's party searched a broad area in the vicinity where Jack Phillips had reported *Titanic* to be. But like Grimm's earlier well-publicized searches for the Loch Ness Monster, Big Foot and Noah's Ark, this one was unsuccessful. Grimm and Harris returned to the area in 1981 and again in 1983, but bad weather and sea conditions (and not looking in the correct place) meant they found nothing.

Success was finally achieved, not by publicity- or treasure-hunters, but by marine geologist Robert Ballard of the prestigious Woods Hole Oceanographic Institution in Massachusetts. Ballard had dreamed of locating *Titanic* as far back as 1973, not only for the knowledge that could be gained, but as a means of testing new developments in underwater photography. By the mid-1980s, he was the head of Woods Hole's Deep Submergence Laboratory, and his group had developed an underwater video camera vehicle named *Argo* and was working on a small, remote-controlled deep-sea robot called *Jason*. Intrigued by the possibilities of this equipment, the US Office of Naval Research agreed to fund a three-week test of *Argo*, which would be used in a search for *Titanic*.

In 1985, Ballard's team and researchers from the Institut français de recherche pour l'exploitation des la mer (IFREMER, or The French Research

Institute for Exploitation of the Sea) under Jean-Louis Michel joined together. They began with a month aboard the French research vessel *Le Suroit*, using a new French side-scanning sonar system to make detailed sweeps over a 240-square-kilometre (150-square-mile) area to the south and east of *Titanic*'s last stated position. The criss-cross pattern they followed became known aboard ship as "mowing the lawn". They covered approximately 80 per cent of the designated area, but found nothing before having to leave to attend to other scientific projects.

LEFT: *The Woods Hole Oceanographic Institution research vessel* Knorr. *The remotely controlled vehicle* Hercules *– a successor to* Argo *– is being brought aboard after a dive off Sicily in 2003.*

ABOVE: *Jack Grimm (left) with Bill Ryan of Lamont-Doherty Geological Observatory, Columbia University, aboard* Gyre *in 1981. They are shown with a magnetometer, a sensing device to be used on the ocean floor.*

THE ARGO SYSTEM

The discovery of *Titanic* was the culmination of Ballard's development of a remotely controlled, deep-sea visual-imaging system. Designed by Stu Harris of Woods Hole's Deep Submergence Laboratory, by 1985 *Argo* had a steel frame some 4.5 metres (15 feet) long, one metre (3.5 feet) wide, one metre high and weighing 1.8 tonnes (two tons).

It was equipped with a series of lights, several components to determine its positioning and three video cameras recording at different scales and covering different angles, the images from which were instantly relayed to a control centre on the ship.

ROBERT BALLARD'S PLEA

At the press conference following the discovery of *Titanic*, Ballard expressed his hopes that the historic ship be treated with dignity and respect, rather than being plundered. "The *Titanic* itself lies in 13,000 feet [4,000 metres] of water on a gently sloping, alpine-like countryside overlooking a small canyon below," he said. "There is no light at this great depth and little light can be found. It is quiet and peaceful and a fitting place for the remains of this greatest of sea tragedies to rest. May it forever remain that way and may God bless these found souls."

TOP LEFT: *The men who found* Titanic. *From left: Jean Jarry, the French project leader; Robert Ballard of Woods Hole and Jean-Louis Michel, who co-led the expedition at sea with Ballard.*

ABOVE: *A sign that was created aboard* Knorr *in honour of her successful search for* Titanic *in 1985. It was signed by both the American and French members of the expedition.*

TOP RIGHT: *This small collection from the thousands of dishes aboard* Titanic *tells a bit of the tragic tale of how even the strongest and richest efforts of man cannot overcome Nature.*

Much of the team then transferred to the Woods Hole research vessel *Knorr*. The operation continued, using the sonar and underwater video cameras aboard *Argo*. For two weeks *Argo* was hauled back and forth, but nothing was found, even when the search area was extended farther east. But early in the morning of 1 September, the watch monitoring the images from *Argo* began to see man-made wreckage, and then a vast boiler appeared. There could be no doubt about it – they had found *Titanic*.

In the following two days, a storm blew in, with winds gusting up to 40 knots and waves of 4 metres (14 feet) smashing against *Knorr*. But *Argo* continued to transmit pictures from 4 kilometres (2.5 miles) below, and at the end of the long debris field the investigators found the bow of the ship,

sitting upright on the ocean floor. With time running out fast before *Knorr* had to go to another scientific project, they carefully guided *Argo*'s passes over the sunken ship, knowing that if the cable to the surface snagged on any of *Titanic*'s features the invaluable piece of equipment could be lost forever.

On their final day, Ballard sent down *Angus*, an unmanned sled with an array of still cameras, and it snapped thousands of pictures of the ship - the bow, the debris field and, at the far end of the debris, 600 metres (1,970 feet) away, what careful analysis would later reveal to be the stern.

Ballard and company then turned regretfully back towards Woods Hole, not yet realizing that they had only experienced the first step in the new existence of *Titanic*.

ABOVE: *The bow of* Titanic *silhouetted by the spotlight from the* Mir 2 *submersible, which was sitting at the time on the anchor crane of the ship's foredeck.*

THE EXPLORATION OF TITANIC

Robert Ballard now knew exactly where *Titanic* was located, and in 1986 he led another expedition, this time to explore the great wreck. His efforts were again primarily funded by the Office of Naval Research, with an official goal of testing *Jason Junior* (or *JJ*), the prototype of the Deep Submergence Laboratory's remote-controlled underwater robot with photographic capabilities. Meanwhile, the French withdrew from the project after the initial images of *Titanic* were released by Woods Hole before IFREMER received them.

In July, Ballard's party was taken to the *Titanic* site aboard *Atlantis II*. Over a period of 12 days they made ten dives in *Alvin*, a research submersible modified to sustain the pressure of great depths and to house *JJ* on its bow. Each dive took up to ten hours, including two and a half to descend some 4,000 metres (13,000 feet) and the same to return to the surface.

The first dive had to be severely curtailed owing to a salt-water leak into the battery pack that powered *Alvin*. Ballard and two colleagues had

just enough time to locate *Titanic*'s bow, which suddenly loomed through the darkness in front of them like a monstrous wall of black steel rising straight from the seabed. It was the first time human beings had seen *Titanic* itself in almost three-quarters of a century. They then ascended to avert the potential technical disaster in the sub, but the sight had been enough to drive the programme full-speed ahead in the ensuing days.

The problems with *Alvin* were soon resolved, and on the second dive Ballard and his team landed

ABOVE: *An underwater research robot used by IFREMER during the increasingly competitive investigation of* Titanic.

THE FATE OF TITANIC'S BOW

Ballard's investigation answered many questions about how *Titanic* broke up. As the sinking bow forced the stern higher out of the water, the ship finally snapped between the third and fourth funnels, a structural weak point because of its large open spaces, such as an engine room air-shaft and the aft Grand Staircase. The bow followed the angle in which it already pointed, and planed down, gathering speed until it reached the seabed, and burying its nose 18 metres (60 feet) into the sediment. The rest of the bow bent as it settled onto the bottom, and as it did so, the decks near the tear in the hull collapsed upon themselves.

TOP LEFT: JJ *exploring the starboard forecastle deck. Lit up in the little robot's lights is a bollard covered by seven decades' worth of rust and damage caused by iron-eating bacteria.*

ABOVE *The bow section of* Titanic. *It smashed into the seabed with such force that it was buried 18 metres (60 feet), up to the starboard anchor.*

TOP RIGHT: *The portholes for the officers' quarters on the starboard side of* Titanic. *It can be seen from the two-part windows that not only the passengers received a high standard of quality.*

on *Titanic*'s mighty forward deck to find, much to their amazement, that the wood planking was gone; only the metal sub-deck survived. They soon realized that undersea worms and wood-boring molluscs had consumed most of the ship's wood, although some of the harder varieties, such as teak, remained in the interiors. Other softer materials – including paper, cloth and human remains – had also disappeared through the ravages of time and deep-sea organisms. Ballard also investigated the opening above the area where the fore Grand Staircase had stood and the collapsed area at the rear of the bow section.

In the following days, Ballard made an intensive examination of the two major sections of the wreck and the debris field that was between and around them. Key to the success of the operation was Martin Bowen's control of *JJ*. He dropped the small robot, known by some as the "swimming eyeball", down the Grand Staircase as far as B deck, and also sent it to explore areas too small or confined for *Alvin* to enter. Meanwhile, *Alvin* and *JJ* between them took thousands of photographs.

The mangled stern was the most distressing area to investigate because they knew so many people had died there, having moved progressively farther back as the bow went under the water. Although it was sitting upright and facing the same direction as the bow, it was a picture of carnage: exploded, fragmented and jumbled.

As with the bow, Ballard hoped to be able to learn from it more about the actual injury caused by the iceberg. But like the bow, it was buried too deeply to allow an exact determination of the extent of any damage.

Between the two major portions of *Titanic* was a field of debris almost 610 metres (2,000 feet) long. There were thousands upon thousands of items littering the bottom, including lumps of coal; metal objects such as heaters, pots and pans, wrought-iron benches, bedsprings and the ship's safes; and all manner of non-metallic materials, such as bathtubs, floor tiles, bottles, statues from public rooms, plates and cups and numerous passenger effects.

When *Atlantis II* ran out of time, Ballard and company turned back towards the US. It had been a sobering experience, but Ballard was pleased to think that, because of the condition *Titanic* was in, it was at least impossible to salvage her. However, there were others who had entirely different thoughts.

TOP: *Divers work to raise items taken from the debris field in the vicinity of the two large sections of* Titanic *to the surface. Thousands of items have now been collected from the deep waters.*

THE SINKING OF THE STERN

The stern of *Titanic* did not sink as quickly as the bow, which had already filled with water. But as it descended, the force of the water rushing in pushed out the air, the violence ripping open the poop deck and thrusting it backwards onto itself. Dropping more or less straight down, it slammed into the seabed so hard that it was buried to about 14 metres (45 feet) at the rudder. The force of hitting the bottom caused the decks to collapse onto one another and the outside plating to crumple and bulge outwards.

TOP RIGHT: *The stern section of* Titanic. *The stern appears more damaged than the bow, because it dropped more or less straight-down instead of planning. It then hit the seabed with such violence that it was buried 14 metres (45 feet) at points.*

ABOVE: *The remains of a deck bench — the wood attached to it long since consumed by undersea creatures — was discovered in the debris field near the wreck of* Titanic.

THE SALVAGE OF TITANIC

O nce Robert Ballard's team discovered *Titanic*'s location, it was apparent that the wreck would prove an irresistible draw for those wishing to study it, photograph it or retrieve artefacts. The following year, Titanic Ventures, of Connecticut, USA, teamed up with Ballard's former French partner, the IFREMER to conduct scientific studies, make photographic records and engage in recovery operations on *Titanic*. Over two months, 23 dives were made from IFREMER's ship *Nadir* in the submersible *Nautile*, during which some 1,800 artefacts were taken from the debris field and the wreck itself. Unfortunately, it has been argued that the care normally shown at significant archaeological sites was not taken during the examination, and some damage to *Titanic* occurred – such as when the crow's nest bell was pulled from the mast, in the process of which the crow's nest itself collapsed.

The retrieval of items from the ship caused enormous controversy, and efforts were made in the US Congress to prevent such operations, but, as *Titanic* lies in international waters, such efforts came to nothing. Many of the objects gathered in 1987 were put on display in a series of exhibitions around Europe, but the promise of the organizations involved to treat the artefacts with dignity was called into question when some of

them appeared in *Return to the Titanic ... Live*, a sensationalized French television show inexplicably hosted by American actor Telly Savalas, who showed little knowledge of *Titanic*.

In 1991, a joint Russian–Canadian expedition spent three weeks filming *Titanic* for what eventually became the IMAX movie *Titanica*. The next year, a new company, Marex-Titanic, Inc., set off on a salvage operation, but Titanic Ventures went to court to stop the effort, launching several years of legal wrangling. In 1993, RMS Titanic, Inc. acquired the assets and liabilities of Titanic Ventures, and thereupon launched a new expedition in conjunction with IFREMER. Making 15 dives, they brought back some 800 artefacts, including a set of the ship's whistles and one of the lifeboat davits.

Some of the items collected in 1993 were introduced into a court with maritime jurisdiction in Virginia, and the following year a US district court declared RMS Titanic, Inc. the salvor-in-possession of the wreck and entire *Titanic* site. This ruling excluded anyone else from visiting the site to gather artefacts, and has limited operations of others to filming or viewing the ship and location. Since that ruling, RMS Titanic, Inc. has conducted another five expeditions, the first three in conjunction with IFREMER. In 1994, 700

ABOVE: *The bell of* Titanic, *which was recovered from the ship's wreckage. It went on display at the National Maritime Museum in Greenwich in 1994.*

WHAT SURVIVORS SAID

Like the general public, *Titanic* survivors who were still alive when the salvage began had a wide range of views about the operations. Eva Hart was one of the most outspoken critics. "The ship is its own memorial. Leave it there," she said, adding that it was her father's grave, and "you don't go poking around in someone's grave". But Beatrice Sandström wrote that, "I am personally pleased … Your presentation of the recovered objects from the ship will help to teach the present and future generations the timeless human lessons learned from this great marine tragedy."

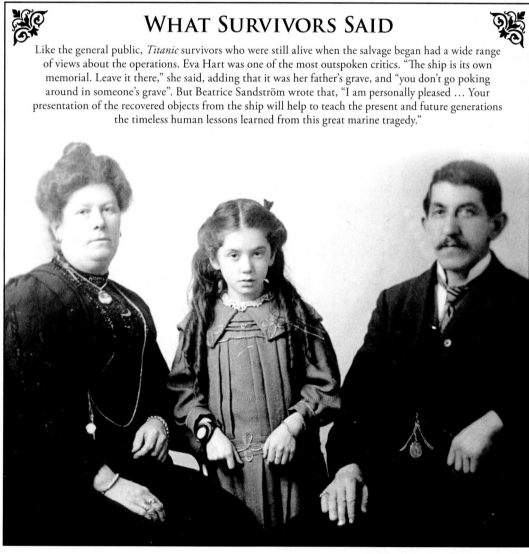

TOP: *The giant starboard wing propeller from* Titanic *– one of the great feats of engineering of its time – now lies partially buried in the seabed under the Atlantic Ocean.*

ABOVE: *Three-quarters of a century after seven-year-old Eva Hart boarded* Titanic *with her parents, she vehemently criticized the collection of artefacts from the ship's wreckage. She died in 1996 at the age of 91.*

TITANIC

TOP: *One of the deckchairs from Titanic. The key to the binocular store for the Titanic's crow's nest. The key sold for 130,000 euros at auction in 2007.*

BOX: *Allan Carlin, general counsel for RMS Titanic Inc with the "Big Piece", the largest section of Titanic that has actually been able to be brought to the surface and then to land.*

RIGHT: *Millvina Dean opens a Titanic exhibition in Southampton. Only two months old when she was saved with her mother and brother, she was the last of the survivors of Titanic to die in 2009.*

more artefacts were gathered, as well as more than 170 pieces of coal, some of which have since been sold. Two years later, efforts were made to answer some of the questions about the disaster by taking an international team of biologists, naval architects, historians and metallurgists to examine the wreck and conduct a broad range of investigations into the remains. RMS Titanic, Inc. also conducted expeditions in 1998, 2000 and 2004.

After the early controversy, the salvage issue became less objectionable to much of the public after the National Maritime Museum in Greenwich, England, agreed to stage an exhibition of artefacts. Entitled "The Wreck of the *Titanic*", it opened in October 1994 with a ceremonial ribbon-cutting involving two survivors, Mrs Edith Brown Haisman and Miss Millvina Dean. The exhibition proved so popular that it was extended for six months and was viewed by approximately 750,000 people.

Despite the success of the exhibitions at the National Maritime Museum and other museums around the world, there remain many who still feel it inappropriate to gather artefacts from what they believe to be a gravesite. The managers of RMS Titanic, Inc. insist that the operation will protect, conserve and restore the recovered artefacts, in the process helping the public learn about and understand *Titanic* and her place in history. As with so many other debates or questions about *Titanic*, this argument is likely to rumble on.

THE BIG PIECE

Knowing that it was impossible to raise the bow or stern of *Titanic*, in 1996 RMS Titanic, Inc. focused on a separate, 17-ton section of the hull nicknamed the "Big Piece". The Big Piece was raised to 61 metres (200 feet) below the surface by means of diesel-filled flotation bags, and the expedition ship *Nadir* attempted to haul it to New York. Two days later, the cables holding the Big Piece failed, and it resank. In 1998, it was raised again, this time to the surface, and attached to the ship *Abeille Supporter*. It has been exhibited in the US and extensively treated for preservation.

ABOVE: *After several years of preparatory efforts in 1998 the "Big Piece", a 15-tonne (17-ton) section of* Titanic's *hull, was brought to Boston. It has since been exhibited and considerable conservation and research has been carried out.*

❦ THE UNSINKABLE SHIP ❦

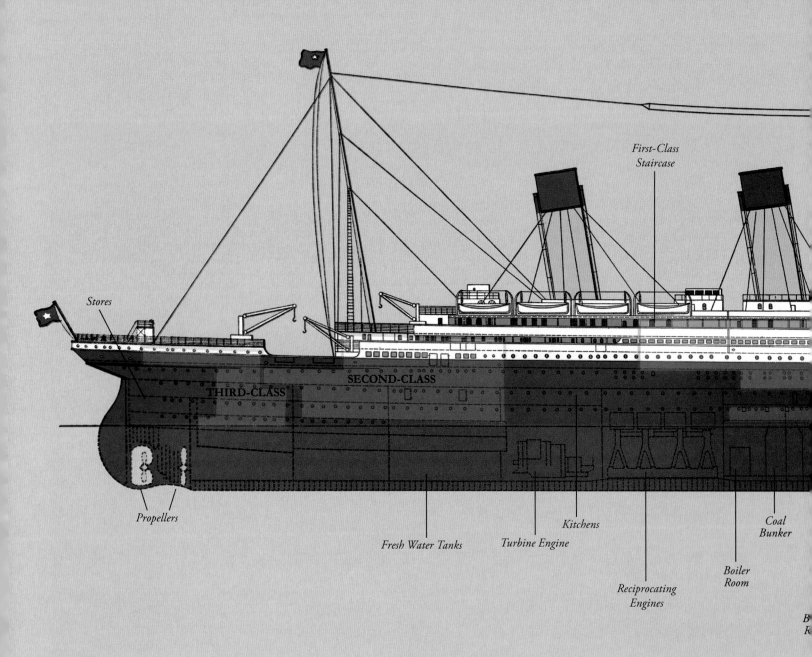

First-Class
Staircase

Stores

THIRD-CLASS

SECOND-CLASS

Propellers

Fresh Water Tanks

Kitchens

Turbine Engine

Coal
Bunker

Boiler
Room

Reciprocating
Engines

ABOVE: *A drawing of* Titanic *showing many of the main sections of the ship. The magnificent forward first-class staircase was perhaps the most famous internal feature, but, intriguingly, it was not part of the original concept. Initially, there was to be a three-deck first-class dining room, but this spectacular feature was eventually replaced as the grand focal point by the staircase.*

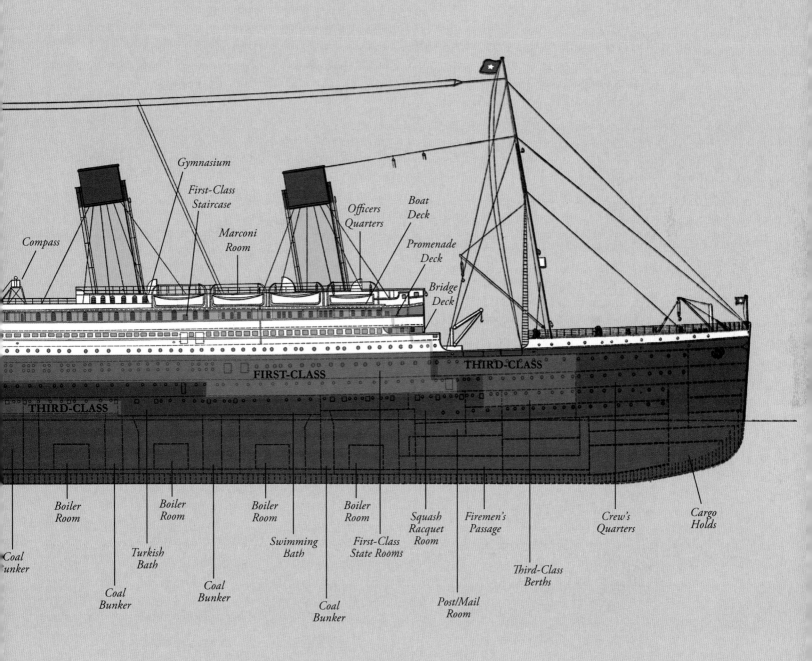

Gymnasium

First-Class
Staircase

Officers
Quarters

Boat
Deck

Marconi
Room

Compass

Promenade
Deck

Bridge
Deck

FIRST-CLASS

THIRD-CLASS

THIRD-CLASS

Boiler
Room

Boiler
Room

Boiler
Room

Boiler
Room

Squash
Racquet
Room

Firemen's
Passage

Crew's
Quarters

Cargo
Holds

Coal
Bunker

Turkish
Bath

Swimming
Bath

First-Class
State Rooms

Third-Class
Berths

Coal
Bunker

Coal
Bunker

Coal
Bunker

Post/Mail
Room

TITANIC REMEMBERED

No other shipwreck in history has made such an indelible imprint upon the imagination as that of *Titanic*. The events of the tragedy never truly left the consciousness of the Western public, but the excitement generated by Robert Ballard's discovery of *Titanic*'s resting place, and then the huge success of James Cameron's blockbuster film of 1997, have made certain that the tale will continue to fascinate people throughout the world.

Just as happens today, immediately after the tragedy several books were hastily produced to capitalize on public interest. A more thoughtful and serious work was *The Truth About the Titanic*, written by historian Archibald Gracie, a first-class passenger who corresponded with other survivors to collect a broad range of information and opinion. But sadly, he did not live to see its popular reception, dying in December 1912 aged only 53, having never fully recovered from swimming to the overturned Collapsible B and staying atop it all night in wet, freezing clothes.

At the same time, second-class passenger Lawrence Beesley, who had escaped on Lifeboat 13, produced *The Loss of the SS* Titanic: *Its Story and Its Lessons,* which has long been considered one of the most insightful, informative and reasoned accounts. Since the works by Gracie and Beesley, more than 850 books about the disaster

have appeared, as well as innumerable articles. More than a dozen films have also told parts of the story, the first starring and co-written by 22-year-old silent movie star Dorothy Gibson, who had survived in Lifeboat 7. Released on 14 May 1912, less than a month after *Titanic* sank, it was given outstanding reviews by film trade magazines, but was widely criticized elsewhere for being insensitive to those who had lost loved ones. Such lack of feeling was nothing, however, when compared to a version three decades later made under the auspices of Nazi propaganda minister Joseph Goebbels, and showing the true hero to be a German passenger.

What is frequently considered the best film of the tragedy was *A Night to Remember,* which appeared in 1958 based on a book of the same name, and starred Kenneth More as Second Officer Charles Lightoller and David McCallum

ABOVE: *Leonardo DiCaprio and Kate Winslet are confronted with the flooding of the area around the first-class staircase in James Cameron's* Titanic.

TITANIC: THE MUSICAL

The tragedy of *Titanic* is not something that one might normally consider appropriate to sing about, but the difficulties facing such a proposition were overcome in 1997 when *Titanic: The Musical* opened on Broadway. Although plagued early on with technical problems and criticized for its story-line before it even opened, the musical became a huge success and ran at the Lunt-Fontanne Theatre for 804 performances. Despite taking great liberties with the facts (including who lived and died), it broke box office records for 15 consecutive weeks before winning five Tony Awards, including Best Musical.

as wireless operator Harold Bride. But none of these could match the financial success of Cameron's version with Kate Winslet and Leonardo DiCaprio. In the following years, Cameron followed up by making numerous dives to the remains of the ship, culminating in the IMAX film *Ghosts of the Abyss*, which featured extensive footage of the wreck.

Cameron's film initiated the largest wave yet of interest in *Titanic*. Memorabilia of all forms has been produced in recent years and, along with original posters, photos, books and other items, has made *Titanic* a booming business.

No aspect of this is more widespread than the postal stamps that were produced throughout the world. Enthusiasts have been able to purchase stamps featuring *Titanic* (although many include inaccurate representations of the ship or events) from countries as diverse as Angola, the Bahamas, Barbados, Eire (The Republic of Ireland), Gambia, Grenada, Guyana, Kyrgystan, Liberia, Madagascar, the Maldives, Mali, Niger, Romania, Russia, Sierra Leone, St Vincent and the Grenadines, the United Kingdom, the United States and the former Yugoslavia.

Similarly, there are societies and clubs around the world dedicated to *Titanic*. The foremost is the *Titanic* Historical Society,

founded in 1963 by Edward S Kamuda, and maintaining the *Titanic* Museum in Indian Orchard, Massachusetts. The society has thousands of members drawn from all over the world, many conducting research into the ship, her passengers and her tragic voyage. The museum features such items as the ship's original blueprints from Harland & Wolff, Frederick Fleet's discharge book and the life-jacket worn by Madeleine Astor.

Keeping up with technology, there are also innumerable websites devoted to *Titanic*, compiling all of the known material on the subject and encouraging discussion. Through all of these efforts, the memories of *Titanic* and the disaster that befell her are preserved.

ABOVE LEFT: *A poster advertising the 1958 film* A Night to Remember, *which is still widely considered the best film ever made about the tragedy.*

TOP RIGHT: Titanic: The Musical *opened in April 1997 to great scepticism from the critics.*

ABOVE RIGHT: *The* Titanic *Museum in Indian Orchard, Massachusetts holds a host of exciting artefacts from the doomed ship.*

THE ENDURING LEGACY

T he individual bravery and heroism shown by those who died on *Titanic* caught the spirit of the age in the final years before the Great War, a time when sacrifice for God, country, mankind's progress or a noble ideal was still most honourable – and honoured. Before long, many memorials – statues, plaques, church windows, fountains, even entire buildings or structures – were dedicated to those individuals and groups of people who lost their lives when *Titanic* went down.

Nowhere were the dead more universally mourned than in Britain, and in no city more so than Southampton, the home of a large percentage of the crew. There, in 1914, a magnificent tribute to *Titanic*'s engineers was dedicated in East Park. A different Southampton memorial honoured the ship's postal workers, another the musicians and yet another the stewards, sailors and firemen. Liverpool, the official home of the White Star Line, also built multiple memorials, and numerous towns created cenotaphs by which to remember their native sons, including orchestra leader Wallace Hartley in Colne, Lancashire, shipbuilder Thomas Andrews in Comber, County Down, Northern Ireland and, across the Atlantic, Major Archibald Butt in Augusta, Georgia. The most extravagant building prompted by the disaster is the Harry Elkins Widener Memorial Library

at Harvard, financed by Eleanor Widener in memory of her son.

Despite the many poignant monuments and the numerous books, films and other ways of remembering the tragedy and the individuals who died in it, the greatest legacy of *Titanic* was the worldwide legislation it prompted to establish safer sea travel. Both the American and British inquiries demanded that new safety regulations be put in place, and soon thereafter ships were required to carry enough lifeboats to hold everyone aboard, to conduct lifeboat drills and, for those with 50 or more people, to have a 24-hour radio watch. The public reaction to the tragedy also forced the governments most heavily involved in Atlantic shipping to take action; not long after the disaster, shipping lanes were shifted south, away from the ice. In addition, international meetings relating to safety at sea were scheduled.

Meanwhile, the US Navy assigned two cruisers to patrol the Northwest Atlantic in the general region of the Grand Banks, where *Titanic* had sunk, and keep shipping informed of ice. The next year, the Navy was unable to perform this function, so it was taken over by the US Revenue Cutter Service, the forerunner of the US Coast Guard. This safety measure proved so successful that when the first International Conference on the Safety of Life at Sea was convened in London in late 1913, the major maritime nations joined to create the International Ice Patrol (IIP). The functions assigned to the IIP were to patrol the Northwest Atlantic during the season of iceberg

ABOVE: *A patch worn by members of the US Coast Guard's International Ice Patrol. There have been a number of patches signifying their operation through the years.*

INTERNATIONAL CONVENTION FOR SAFETY OF LIFE AT SEA

One of the major triumphs of the London conference in 1913 was the agreement on the International Convention for Safety of Life at Sea (SOLAS), which came into force the next year. An updated second version was adopted in 1929, a third in 1940, a fourth in 1960 and the current one in 1974. SOLAS has wide-ranging provisions, specifying minimum standards for the construction, equipment and operation of ships. Numerous amendments have been made to SOLAS 1974, in order to keep abreast of technological developments and make ships as safe as possible.

danger, monitor and track icebergs in that region, provide information to shipping about the limits of known ice and attempt to keep the transatlantic lanes clear.

Following the experience gained in 1912 and 1913, this task was turned over to the US Coast Guard, with expenses initially shared among the 13 nations most heavily involved in transatlantic navigation. In recent years, the governments contributing to the operation have included Belgium, Canada, Denmark, Finland, France, Germany, Greece, Italy, Japan, the Netherlands, Norway, Panama, Poland, Spain, Sweden, the United Kingdom and the US.

The US Coast Guard has continued to operate the IIP for nine decades, with the exception of the years during the two world wars. Today, the IIP makes regular surveillance flights from Hercules HC-130 aircraft and combines the information obtained with that from all ships operating in or passing through the ice area. Data relating to icebergs, ocean currents and winds allow for the twice-daily projection of iceberg locations and ice limits over the radio and internet. As a result, since the inception of the IIP, no loss of life or property has occurred because of a collision with an iceberg in the area monitored.

TITANIC MEMORIALS

There are many memorials in 21 different countries to the individuals or groups of people lost aboard *Titanic*. Among the most notable are:

Thomas Andrews Memorial Hall: Comber, County Down, Northern Ireland, UK
Major Archibald Butt Memorial Bridge: Augusta, Georgia, USA
Father Thomas Byles Memorial Window: St Helen's Church, Ongar, Essex, England, UK
Crew, Stewards, Sailors and Firemen Memorial Fountain: Southampton, England, UK
Engineers Memorial: Liverpool, England, UK
Engineers Memorial: Southampton, England, UK
Wallace Hartley Memorial: Colne, Lancashire, England, UK
William Murdoch Memorial: Dalbeattie, Dumfries & Galloway, Scotland, UK
Musicians Memorial: Liverpool, England, UK
Musicians Memorial: Southampton, England, UK
John Phillips Memorial Cloister: Godalming, Surrey, England, UK
Postal Workers Memorial: Southampton, England, UK
Captain Edward Smith Memorial: Lichfield, Staffordshire, England, UK
Isador and Ida Straus Memorial Fountain: New York, USA
Titanic Memorial: Belfast, Northern Ireland, UK
Titanic Memorial: Cobh, Eire (Republic of Ireland)
Titanic Memorial Lighthouse: New York, USA
Harry Elkins Widener Memorial Library: Cambridge, Massachusetts, USA
Women's *Titanic* Memorial: Washington DC, USA

ABOVE: *A contemporary piece of art commemorating the loss of* Titanic. *This one, which emphasizes the British and American passengers and crew, is made of woven silk.*

ABOVE RIGHT: *United States Coast Guard cutter (USCGC)* Evergreen *was first commissioned in 1942, and in 1963 she became an oceanographic vessel for the International Ice Patrol, a function she served for 19 years. She was decommissioned in 1990.*

CREDITS

The publishers would like to thank the following sources for their kind permission to reproduce the pictures in this book.
Key, t: top, b: bottom, l: left, r: right.

AKG LONDON: 93t

ALAMY IMAGES: /James Hughes: 86

CORBIS: /Aldridge & Sons Auction: 166r, /Bettmann: 10, 44tr, 50b, 69, 80t, 89tl, 90tl, 90l, 90r, 107l, 109, 138, 140b, 107,/Christie's Images: 24, /Fine Art Photographic Library: 12-13, /Angelo Hornak: 146r, /The Mariners' Museum: 8-9, 14-15, 168-169, Underwood & Underwood: 111b, 111r, /Ralph White: 30c, 146l, 160, 161, 162, 163t, 163b, 163t

FATHER BROWNE S.J. COLLECTION: f-end, 25b, 44tl, 45b, 48, 49, 60t, 61, 62, 61t, 62b, 63t, 87

GETTY IMAGES: 11, 27b, 41b, 89, 94, 67, 115t, 130, 109, 139, 145, / AFP: 166bl, /Aurora: 156, /Michel Boutefeu: 9, National Geographic: 154-155, 159, /Time & Life Pictures: 62t, 134, /Topical Press Agency: b-end, /Roger Viollet: 107

INTERNATIONAL ICE PATROL: 172, 173tr,

PAINTING BY KEN MARSCHALL © 1977: 82-83

MARY EVANS PICTURE LIBRARY: 12tl, 16, 17b, 49t, 63b, 65tl, 71r, 92, 93l, 110r, /Illustrated London News Ltd: 46-47, 70, 85, 94l, 97t, /Onslow Auctions Limited: 6, 28, 45, 40, 112, 173tl

NATIONAL ARCHIVES: 143t

NATIONAL GEOGRAPHIC STOCK: /Emory Kristof: 161r

NATIONAL MARITIME MUSEUM, GREENWICH: 108

PRESS ASSOCIATION: 165, 65tr, 80, 95, 135bl, /Diane Bondareff: 166l, Joan Marcus: 171t, /Topham: 83, 107tc, 107tr, 113t, 144

PRIVATE COLLECTION: 40

REX FEATURES: /Boston Herald: 167, /Everett Collection: 171l, / Nils Jorgensen: 164, /Sipa Press: 158l, 158b

SOMCHITH VONGPRACHANH: 29, 41, 91, 97b

TITANIC HISTORICAL SOCIETY INC & TITANIC MUSEUM: 79b, 106, 171c

TOPFOTO.CO.UK: 12tr, 12bl, 19l, 42, 65b, 67r, 79, 80bl, 88, 90bl, 93br, 114, 115b, 132-133, 140t, 141, 143b, 147, 158r, 165, ARPL/HIP/: 60, British Library/HIP: 135r, /PA Photos: 68, 166br, /Public Record Office /HIP: 67l, /Ullstein Bild: 30t, 30-31b, 61b, 80br, 84, 85l, 96, 104, 170, /World History Archive: 110l

ULSTER FOLK & TRANSPORT MUSEUM: 18t, 18b, 19r, 22-23, 26, 27t, 38, 39, 168

Envelope credits:
1: Underwood & Underwood/Corbis Images
2, 4: Getty Images
3: Time & Life Picture/Getty Images
5: De Agostini/Getty Images
6: Everett Collection/Rex Features

Every effort has been made to acknowledge correctly and contact the source and/or copyright holder of each picture and Imagine Publishing apologises for any unintentional errors or omissions, which will be corrected in future editions of this book.

FACSIMILE CREDITS
With kind permission of:
© Corbis: /Reuters: item 49

© Fr Browne SJ Collection/Irish Picture Library: item 12

© Getty Images: /SSPL: item 26

© Mary Evans Picture Library: /Illustrated London News Ltd: items 14 & 27; /Onslow Auctions Limited: items 10 & 15; /The National Archives, London: item 50

© The National Archives of the UK (P.R.O.), Kew: items 9, 11, 13, 30–31, 38, 39, 42, 43, 44, 45–46, 47

© National Maritime Museum, Greenwich, London: item 28

© New York Archives, National Archives & Records Administration Archive: items 8, 29

© Robert Opie: item 6

© Topfoto.co.uk: /The Grainger Collection: items 15 & 48; /PressNet: item 16

© Ulster Folk & Transport Museum, (National Museums Northern Ireland):
items 1, 2, 12, 15–20

© US National Archives & Records Administration Archive: items 25, 40A & 40B, 41

ACCOUNTS:
© National Maritime Museum, Greenwich, UK: 8, 31, 44, 45, 61, 63, 66, 69, 71, 78, 81, 86, 89, 91, 95, 96, 106, 107, 109, 110 top, 113, 115, 130, 140, 141 143, 147

© US Board of Inquiry: 110 bottom

© US Senate: 147 right

© BBC Titanic Archive: 28

❖ PROPELLER ❖

ABOVE: The massive, manganese-bronze centre propeller of *Titanic* prior to its installation. Cast in one piece, this 20-tonne (22-ton) giant was approximately 5 meters (exactly 16 feet, 6 inches) across.

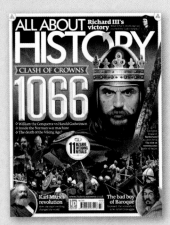

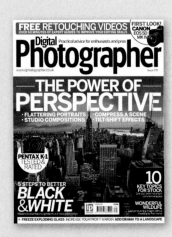

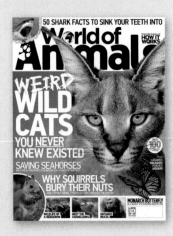

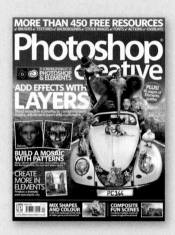

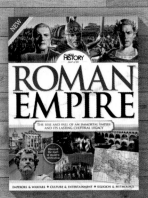

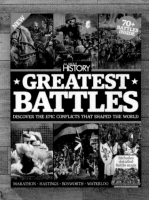
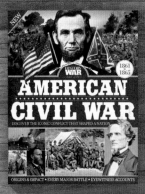

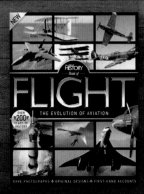